BLESSING AND GLORY AND THANKSGIVING

William R. Blott

Blessing and glory and thanksgiving
The growth of a Canadian liturgy

 A Liturgy Canada book

Published and distributed by

 Anglican Book Centre
Toronto, Canada

1998 **Liturgy Canada**

Copyright © 1998 by Liturgy Canada

Book design, typesetting: Willem Hart Art & Design Inc.

Canadian Cataloguing in Publication Data

Blott, William

Blessing and Glory and Thanksgiving: the growth of a Canadian liturgy

Includes bibliographical references

ISBN 1-55126-184-7

1. Anglican Church of Canada – Liturgy. I. Title.

BX5616.B56 1998   264' - 03'00971   C97-930030-4

Published and distributed by
Anglican Book Centre
600 Jarvis Street
Toronto, Ontario
Canada M4Y 2J6

Table of contents

Preface

In the calendar of the *Book of Common Prayer* (1959) Canada, September third is set aside to commemorate the celebration by Robert Wolfall of the "first recorded Anglican Communion Service in Canada." In 1578, on Frobisher's ship off Baffin Island, a little group of Englishmen, visitors in a foreign land, lifted their hearts and voices to God according to the form authorized by their distant queen, Elizabeth I.

In the centuries that followed, many people would come to this country; at first, like Frobisher's crew, they came as expatriates, but as years and generations passed, Canada would become their native land. As they made Canada their home, it was only natural for the feeling to grow that their church and *Prayer Book* should undergo the same process of indigenization that they were experiencing. Just as the changes in their lives had involved much careful consideration, many misgivings, disagreements, and heartache, so too would their *Prayer Book* in subsequent efforts to assimilate and revise it. No part of the revision would be undertaken lightly, but the eucharist, because it lay at the very heart of their faith and because its form and use defined them, was the touchstone and, often enough, a stumbling block in the work. For this reason, the process of liturgical revision in Canada may be looked at most revealingly through the lens of the eucharist.

The actual work of the revision committees forms the skeleton of this process. The Canadian book's distinctive shape and character, however, are also the result of the church's history and the events surrounding the times in which the work proceeded. Thus, in order to fully appreciate what was achieved, it will be helpful to look at the roots of Prayer Book revision and to *tell the story* before appraising the outcome.

One of the oddities in this long process is the absence of any women in the story. The reason for this has nothing to do with their ability, the value of or commitment to their work in the church. It has to do with what was, generally, an accepted division of labour between men and women in the historical period under study. This demarcation was already seen by some to be ironic, but had only begun to be challenged.

Telling the story of the very human struggles involved in *Prayer Book* revision is the purpose of this book. My aim is to provide ordinary Anglicans with an understanding of, and appreciation for, the way they have worshipped over the years and why they have done it in the various ways they have. At the same time, extensive references are provided to enable those who wish to do so to investigate more fully the history of Canadian liturgy.

In the Preface to the work he and others produced, Archbishop Howard Clark wrote that "this *Book of Common Prayer* is offered to the Church, with the hope that those who use it may become more truly what they already are: the People of God, that New Creation in Christ which finds its joy in adoration of the Creator and Redeemer of all." This book is offered as an aid in that process.

William R. Blott
Toronto, December 1997

1

The English background to revision

Until 1970, Prayer Book revision in the Anglican Church of Canada, as in the Anglican Communion generally, centred on the eucharist.[1] The daily offices of Matins and Evensong had remained substantially unaltered since 1552 and subject to little demand for change. In general, the same may be said for the occasional offices, which took their form between 1552 and 1662, and without substantial change (though some changes were significant) continued to be accepted. The Ministry to the Sick was indeed altered fundamentally in 1962, but this was the exception to the rule. The eucharist, however, was a focus of attention, and often controversy, since its first English form appeared in 1549.

The historical reasons for this controversy emanated from a growing dissatisfaction with a decadent ecclesiastical institution and its mechanical dispensation of grace, and from Martin Luther's passionate assertion that one is saved by faith alone — an assertion which raised the whole question of how persons were to work out their salvation from day to day. The answers proposed to that question broadly divided Christians into two groups. On the one side were the conservatives who maintained that, subsequent to entrance into the Christian community, regular participation in the eucharistic assembly remained the normative way in which one received God's grace to live out the implications of one's baptism; if the old form needed cleansing and restoring, so be it. On the other side were the Reformers whose championship of a living faith over dead works led

---

1. Colin Buchanan, Trevor Lloyd & Harold Miller, editors, Anglican Worship Today (Collins, 1980), pp.20-22.

THE BOOK OF

COMMON PRAYER,

AND ADMINISTRATION OF THE SACRAMENTS, AND OTHER
RITES AND CEREMONIES OF THE CHURCH,
ACCORDING TO THE USE OF

The Church of England:

TOGETHER WITH

THE PSALTER OR PSALMS OF DAVID,

POINTED AS THEY ARE TO BE SUNG OR SAID IN CHURCHES;

AND THE FORM AND MANNER OF MAKING, ORDAINING,
AND CONSECRATING OF

BISHOPS, PRIESTS, AND DEACONS.

OXFORD:

PRINTED AT THE UNIVERSITY PRESS,

For the Society for Promoting Christian Knowledge.

SOLD AT THE SOCIETY'S DEPOSITORY, NORTHUMBERLAND AVENUE,
CHARING CROSS, LONDON.

q Pica 16mo.   Cum Privilegio.

The Prayer Book of 1662 used in Canada before the first revision of 1918.

them to emphasize the intangible. Grace, they believed, came direct and unmediated to those who were ready to receive it. By open-hearted hearing and inward digestion of God's Word, and by attention to earnest exhortation and devout meditation on Christ's passion, the mind of each individual could be made ready and the spirit rise in faith "to meet the Lord in the air," as it were.[1]

Both sides of this controversy were given expression in the successive liturgies prepared for the use of the church in England. And the radical change in the eucharist from 1549 to 1552 was matched by the pendulum swings in doctrine which began under Henry VIII and reached extremes under Edward VI and Mary. By the time of Elizabeth I, any hope of uniting the populace in one belief was gone. At the same time, however, affairs of state demanded a common front against the aggression of Spain from without and against the divisiveness of religious debate within. In the circumstances, the best that could be achieved was an outward show of cohesion and a willingness to tolerate differences in theology.[2] Thus, behind a facade of liturgical uniformity (the 1559 BCP[3]) imposed by law and severely enforced, and within an inclusive general statement of the faith (the Thirty-Nine Articles), both conservatives and Reformers were allowed a good deal of freedom.

Under cover of this rigid but tolerant framework, Reformers began to develop the classical Puritanism based on Calvin's theology and looking to 1552 for its expression, the conservatives — led by Jewel, Whitgift, Hooker, and the Caroline Di-

---

1. In England, Archbishop Cranmer cautiously, but clearly, identified himself with the Reformers. The church he led, in spite of having to use his Prayer Book, continued to have members in both groups.

2. G.M. Trevelyan, Illustrated History of England (London, 1945), p. 325. Trevelyan notes that "many who disliked [Elizabeth's] ecclesiastical compromise as being too Protestant, or not Protestant enough, accepted it as the condition of tranquil government, which in an age of rival fanaticisms seemed, and perhaps was, a miracle of statecraft." Elizabeth, for her part did not wish "to make windows into men's souls." Cf. also Owen Chadwick, The Reformation (Harmondsworth, 1964). p. 129 f.

3. In the 1559 BCP the 1552 black rubric denying Christ's real presence in the Eucharist was removed, and the 1549 words of administration affirming his presence were restored.

vines — developed the distinctive Anglicanism best expressed in 1549 (and its derivatives). At the time of the Restoration in 1660, both theologies were clearly enough enunciated that, by the end of the century, they had been institutionalized in two parties — the Low Church and High Church, respectively. High Church sympathizers, as a result of the radical puritanism experienced during the Commonwealth, were in the ascendant, and the restored Prayer Book might have been of the 1549 model. Parliament, however, wanted no more religious altercations, and the Prayer Book accepted was essentially the 1559 version of the 1552 edition, removed, furthermore, from ecclesiastical control by being entrenched in statute law.

The times had changed — politics, not religion, had become uppermost in public affairs[1] — and for roughly the next 175 years, both old parties were displaced by ecclesiastics who regarded the church as the moral arm of the state and were little interested in either theology or liturgics.

In the nineteenth century, however, the debate between High and Low Churchmen revived. The initiative was taken by the Oxford Movement, which set about with scholarship, enthusiasm, and vigour to restore the catholic heritage of the church. The Low Church party, already working for renewal in the Evangelical Movement, became involved, at first simply to question, and later (outraged by the Ritualists who often credulously translated catholic theology into liturgical practice) to oppose this challenge to the Protestantism that had become widely regarded as the norm of Anglicanism. A good deal of conflict ensued, but through it all the church was slowly, and painfully, working out a new understanding of its nature and position in the world. Inevitably, this process involved the Prayer Book (fixed by law as the vehicle of the church's belief and worship), and the resulting call for revision renewed the old contest between the liturgies of 1549 and 1552.

The way for revision was opened by the creation, in 1854, of a joint committee of the Upper and Lower Houses of the Con-

---

1. Gerald R. Cragg, The Church and the Age of Reason (Harmondsworth, 1970) pp.11-23, 50-72.

vocation of Canterbury, to consider whether the great increase in population over the last half century, and the changed conditions of life brought on by industrialization, necessitated some adaptation of the church's rules in order to meet the spiritual needs of the people. Neither this Committee, nor the Royal Commission on Ritual which succeeded it in 1867, accomplished much in the way of revision. The latter, though, brought forth in 1872 the Act of Uniformity Amended Act (Shortened Services Act), legalizing the separate use of the constituent parts of the Sunday morning liturgy.[1] However, the existence of the Committee and the Royal Commission, by sanctioning revision at the institutional level as opposed to the often anomalistic position of the Ritualists, did encourage the publication of a number of proposals which greatly influenced the course of revision both in England and in Canada.[2]

These proposals took two forms. One set (of which J.M. Neale's in 1856 is an example) called for specific changes: the restoration of the daily offices to the form of 1549 (and hence, by implication, to a similar status); revision of the Lectionary and Calendar; the provision of alternate canticles at Matins; a new Table of Psalms comprehending ferials, holy days, introits, and graduals; in the eucharist, the replacement of the Decalogue by the Kyrie, additional Proper Prefaces, and the reconstruction of the Canon; and generally, more flexibility in the liturgy. Such proposals identified the changes felt necessary in order to make clear the traditional catholic nature of the church.

Other proposals made between 1860 and 1876 helped to establish a framework within which revision would take place

1. *Cranmer had committed the church to a Sunday liturgy consisting of Matins, Litany, and Holy Communion, estimated variously by Whitgift and Hooker to last from one and a half to two hours. This had been continued in the BCP 1662. As early as 1571, however, Archbishop Grindal of York commented on the difficulty of keeping people that long. Cf. Hooker,* Ecclesiastical Polity, *Vol. II (London, 1907) p.133-135. Furthermore, the expectation of people making a weekly communion after generations of weekly mass, but thrice-yearly communion, was an impossible one. In the lax 18th century a solution to both these complaints was achieved by simply allowing people to leave after the sermon.*
2. *A detailed review of the Church of England's progress toward revision of the Prayer Book is given in R.C.D. Jasper,* Prayer Book Revision in England *1800-1900 (London, 1954) p.82 f.*

and the principles by which it would proceed. For example, W. Gresley (who as a student at Oxford in the 1820s had been one of the group with William Palmer and J.H. Newman at Dr. Charles Lloyd's groundbreaking lectures on "The History and Structure of the Anglican Prayer Book") set out two assumptions that he considered fundamental to any consideration of revision: first, that the Prayer Book in substance and spirit be in accord with primitive usage; and second, that, as in the early church, minor details of the liturgy be variable in different places while the broad features remain identical. With these principles for revision, Gresley summed up and brought forward the essential concepts of the Caroline Divines.

Another exemplar of this form of proposal was the anonymous author of the article "Liturgical Revision" in the 1876 issue of *The Church Quarterly Review*, who recognized two other assumptions necessary to Anglicanism: that the Prayer Book be a manual for both the clergy and laity, and that it be used by all groups in the church. Working from these assumptions, he proposed, as principles of revision, that the old goal of absolute conformity must be abandoned, that changes introduced must be optional so as to avoid any taint of party politics, and that any revision should follow the direction of previous ones, which (as R.F. Littledale had already demonstrated) leaned toward the model of 1549.

Littledale, giving expression to these principles, said they would mean five things: no changes would be made simply for the sake of change, no suppression of positive teaching would result, doctrinal alterations would be conservative and restorative, devotional and rubrical changes would seek to achieve greater variety and flexibility, and any omissions would be only of negative and hortatory material whose absence would simplify and elevate the service. The maxim governing all revision should be, wrote the Rev. T. Lathbury (in a phrase which was to become the watchword of the Canadian church) that *adaptation and enrichment were acceptable provided nothing was done contrary to the fundamental principles and practices of the Prayer Book.*

As a result of the corporate and individual initiatives taken toward revision in the nineteenth century, a Royal Commission on Ecclesiastical Discipline was established in 1903. After two years of investigation, the Commission reported two major findings. The first stated that the machinery for governing the church's faith and teaching was defective and in some respects unsuitable.[1] The second concluded that "the law of public worship" was reflective of another age, too narrow for the religious life of the present, and framed in such a way as to deprive the church of "that power of self-adjustment which is inherent in the conception of a living Church."[2] The Commission recommended that the Convocations of Canterbury and York be authorized to consider what changes were needed in the law of worship, and in Letters of Business issued on 10 November 1906, the warrant was issued for them to embark on what was to become the long process of revising the 1662 *Book of Common Prayer*.

---

1. Cf. *Jasper, op. cit.*, *p.57f. and A.O.J.* Cockshut, Anglican Attitudes: A Study of Victorian Religious Controversies *(London, 1959) pp. 41-122.*
2. *Quoted in Alec R.* Vidler, The Church in an Age of Revolution *(Harmondsworth, 1961) p.163.*

2

Prayer Book revision in the United States

While in England efforts at Prayer Book revision seemed to move ahead with all the speed of continental drift, in the United States four revisions took place in less than a century and a half.[1] The reasons for the difference are instructive.

In the first place, after 1776 there was a strong motivation for Americans to make changes. With the Revolution and the subsequent emergence of independent states, it became essential that, at the very least, the state prayers be revised.[2] Thus, initially, Prayer Book revision was forced upon American Anglicans because the status quo was intolerable. The fact that revision went beyond the minimum required, and did not simply respond to the political situation, was due, however, to a new outlook which had grown up in the American colonies themselves. Eighteenth-century American Christians found themselves in a political position analogous to that of sixteenth-century Englishmen, and (as earlier in Europe) a silent revolution in values was taking place to prepare the way and give support to the political reality — the church had become "the ideal of local self-government and of democracy."[3] Even the Anglican Church (a state-supported body until the War of Independence) had come to be popularly seen, and to see itself, as a voluntarist society, independent of political or judicial control, autonomous, and free to go its own way. This philosophy, and the political necessities of post-Revolutionary

1. Massey H. Shepherd Jr., The Oxford American Prayer Book Commentary (New York, 1950) pp. XX-XXIII, presents a succinct outline of the work.
2. Marion J. Hatchett, Sanctifying Life, Time and Space (New York, 1976) p.136f.
3. Lord Acton, Lectures on Modern History (London, 1960) p.192.

America, provided the context in which the idea of liturgical change could be entertained and accepted.

The first revision, the proposed book of 1786, was Latitudinarian in tone, "taking up our Liturgy or Public Service where our former venerable Reformers had been obliged to leave it, and proposing ... further alterations and improvements," as Dr. William Smith, one of its architects, described it.[1] These alterations and improvements, however, occasioned further revision more extensive than might otherwise have been the case, not only by reason of the sharp criticism they received from the English bishops, but also because, coming hard on the ravaging of church membership by the secession of Wesley's followers,[2] they raised apprehensions about the safety of the faith and gave force to the arguments of influential Scottish clergy in several states who were desirous of adopting a model closer to their familiar usage.[3]

A final impulse to revision followed acceptance of the initial work and had the potential to lead to further liturgical development. Though it had to wait some years, the successful work of people like W.R. Muhlenberg, in attracting attention to the condition of American society and its special needs,[4] was particularly fruitful in establishing the concept that liturgy cannot be fixed but must continue to respond to the situation of the society making use of it.[5]

1. *Francis Proctor and W.H. Frere*, A New History of the Book of Common Prayer *(London, 1961) p.238.*
2. *Samuel Eliot Morrison*, The Oxford History of the American People *(New York, 1965) p.293f.*
3. *Hatchett, op. cit., p.152.*
4. *Alonzo Potter*, Memorial Papers *(Philadelphia, 1857) pp.IX-XI, 27-32, 274-289.*
5. *Ibid., pp.113-120.*

3   The Canadian background to revision

I n Canada, when the Anglican Church considered the possibility of revising the Prayer Book at the beginning of the twentieth century, the same theological problems which had frustrated English churchmen had to be faced. A number of factors, though less formally organized than in England, had been at work to create High and Low Church parties, each with wide support and definite opinions about liturgical reform.

Throughout most of the nineteenth century, a great many of the clergy in the Anglican Church of Canada[1] were sympathetic to the catholic revival in England. The early bishops were predominantly High Churchmen of the old school, and during the middle years of the century, there was a great influx of priests trained at Tractarian colleges such as St. Augustine's.[2] These clergy could generally count on the support of the Tory Loyalists, political oligarchs who, favoured from England with the seats of power, formed an influential body in the church.

The Low Church party too, however, drew support from a number of sources. The United Empire Loyalists were not all Tories; many were voluntarists who had brought with them strong democratic tendencies, which led to demands for greater lay involvement in the Church and a distrust, often

---

1. Known at first as The Church of England in Canada, then, after the first General Synod in 1893, as The Church of England in the Dominion of Canada, this body became, in 1955, The Anglican Church of Canada.
2. The rivalry between High and Low Church parties is examined by Christopher Fergus Headon, The Influence of the Oxford Movement Upon the Church of England in Eastern and Central Canada, 1840-1900, an unpublished Doctoral Thesis.

mutual, between themselves and the bishops. Inglis called their outlook "Congregationalism," and while they were not in fact sectarian, many were indeed attracted to the evangelical polity in the church. This attraction was strengthened by a number of contingent factors. One was the presence in the country of a large group of Roman Catholics who, in addition to their disputed faith, were allied by birth and language to England's old enemy, France. Another was the arrival of many Irish, the Protestants amongst whom were strongly Calvinistic in belief. Finally, there was the environment itself: the High view of the church was not only communal in a society with no indigenous roots and no local history of community, but oligarchic and static as well. The Low Church view, by contrast, was individualistic, democratic, fluid, and simple — a view more attuned to the isolation, self-reliance, and catch-as-catch-can nature of frontier life.

During the second half of the nineteenth century, strife between these two parties wracked the church. Contention was often raw and raucous, sometimes with an element of the ludicrous, and mostly occasioned by the introduction of various ceremonies into the liturgy. But none of this made the situation less dangerous. By the 1870s, church leaders of both sides were seeking to establish compromises for fear that continued fighting would extend party divisions to the point of splitting the church. Even so, by that time, fundamental damage had been done with divisions becoming institutionalized in rival seminaries (e.g., Trinity and Wycliffe Colleges), thereby prolonging the survival of party adherence and making more difficult any future rapprochement.

These party battles had a direct bearing on attitudes toward, and the extent of revision to, the Prayer Book. One very great difference between the situation in England and Canada was that, in the former country, the church was established in law and ultimately under the control of the government, whereas in the latter it was, as Archbishop Matheson was to say, "untrammeled ... by State connection."[1] This meant that

---

1. *General Synod*, Journal of Proceedings 1915, *p.15.*

the Anglican Church of Canada was free to do as it wished. But it also meant that there was no third party to whom disputants could turn for a judgment (the Cridge Affair in British Columbia made this explicit[1]), nor, it was realized, was there any limit to what might be done once the principle of revision was endorsed.

Yet by the end of the nineteenth century, even in the vexed field of liturgical reform, some progress had been made. In September of 1851, Bishop G.J. Mountain had called a conference at Quebec of all the bishops of British North America, who there expressed the wish to follow faithfully the doctrine and practice of the Prayer Book, but noted, as well, their belief that the diocesan bishops should have authority to make alterations to meet local needs — specifically, the division of the liturgy into its three component parts and the introduction of an offertory at Matins, so that free-will gifts of money might replace the invidious pew-rents as a means of popular support.

The next step in revision, however, demonstrated the continuing party battles. In 1868, at the second synod of the ecclesiastical Province of Canada (meeting now as an independent and autonomous church), the bishops declined to allow the synod authority to make rubrical changes in the Prayer Book. They did agree, though, that synod could express a resolve as to rubrical meaning. Thus while vestments, candles, altar-cloths, chanting, and genuflecting were deemed tolerable, a resolution was passed stating that elevation, the mixed chalice, and incense were "illegal," and that wafer-bread was "unrubrical."

In 1877, in response to growing demand, the Provincial Synod drew up forms of service for the laying of a cornerstone, the induction of a priest into a parish, and the consecration of a church. There was, however, no revision of present services, but simply the provision of necessary offices not contained in the 1662 Prayer Book.

---

1. H.H. Walsh, The Christian Church in Canada (Toronto, 1956), p. 253. Cf. Philip Carrington, The Anglican Church in Canada (Toronto, 1963) p.150.

Finally, at the Winnipeg Conference of 1890, called to produce a scheme of unity for the whole Canadian church, it was agreed that a General Synod would have jurisdiction in matters of doctrine and worship. Later still, when the first General Synod met in 1893, this authority was hedged about by the Solemn Declaration, which meant, given that synod could not vote to secede from the Anglican Communion, that the church had moved to the point where change could take place in a controlled and orderly fashion.

Thus, there was progress toward liturgical reform, and if progress seems a rather grand word to describe such cautious advance, the circumstances made wariness understandable. Canadian church leaders were not entirely blind to the advantages of liturgical reform, but after the uproar of the late 1800s they were inclined to see it as a Pandora's box.

George Mountain, Bishop of Quebec (left), and John Strachan, Bishop of Toronto (right), expressed the view that the Canadian church was not simply the Church of England in Canada.

Some members of the Central Revision Subcommittee at a meeting in Toronto in September, 1917. Seated (L to R), Bishop Scholfield (British Columbia); Bishop Doull (Kootenay); Bishop Richardson (Fredericton); the Chairman, Bishop Williams (Huron); the Primate, Archbishop Matheson (Rupertsland); the Secretary, Archdeacon Armitage (Halifax); Bishop Roper (Ottawa); Bishop Bidwell (Ontario); Bishop Farthing (Montreal). Standing (L to R), Archdeacon Paterson-Smyth; Rev. Prof. Abbott-Smith; Mr. Charles Jenkins; Rev. Dyson Hague; Archdeacon Cody; Dean Neales; Dean Evans; Mr. Matthew Wilson; Canon Simpson; Rev. Principal Waller; Canon Plumtre.

Matthew Wilson (inset), is significant not only because he was a layman – Wilson, along with J.A. Waller and Kerwin Martin were informed and responsible laity of a model which would be welcome today. (Courtesy Christ Church Chatham, and British and Colonial Press Ltd., Toronto)

4

The first Canadian revision

The beginnings of Prayer Book revision in Canada are worth noting, because they throw light upon the obstacles that lay in the path of revision: the conservatism of the bishops, the separation of people by great distance, the meagerness of funding, and party divisions in the church.

A Compromise Beginning

The first General Synod of the Canadian church prepared itself to deal at the national level with anticipated requests for revision by setting up a standing Joint Committee on Doctrine, Worship, and Discipline; and at the second General Synod in September of 1896, the expected request was made. How revision was treated over the next six years illustrates the conservatism of the bishops.

At the beginning of 1896, Matthew Wilson, Q.C., of Chatham in the Diocese of Huron, had written to Dr. Maurice Baldwin, his bishop, about the desirability of having a Canadian edition of the Prayer Book. Baldwin advised Wilson to bring the idea to the Diocesan Synod in June and that, in the meantime, he would present this idea to the House of Bishops meeting in April.

At the Huron Synod that June, the pattern emerged for what was to follow during the next fifteen years. Baldwin (apparently voicing the opinion of the House of Bishops) suggested in his opening address that "distinctive prayers and offices authorized by the Provincial Synod" be printed in the text of the old book.

Wilson's motion (characterized by Baldwin as "venturesome") asked, however, for "a Prayer Book containing all the prayers or other matter framed for the service of the Church of England in Canada and ... issued with the authority of the General Synod."[1] Where Baldwin envisioned local additions to the generally received corpus, Wilson called for a reconstituted text whose authority would come from its framer: the Canadian church. The Huron Synod decided for the latter and passed on Wilson's motion as a "Memorial" to General Synod.

At General Synod that fall, the memorial was duly referred to the standing Joint Committee on Doctrine, Worship, and Discipline, which reported back the desire not for a revision but for an appendix to the *Book of Common Prayer* containing additional services and prayers made necessary by the Canadian situation: services for the consecration of a church and a church yard, the induction and institution of an incumbent, a thanksgiving at harvest, intercessions for missions, and prayers for various levels of government in church and state. On the one matter which came before it requiring actual revision of a part of the Prayer Book (the Ordering of Deacons), the Committee was unable to do anything since the Upper House "declined to consider this topic."[2] Likewise, at the next General Synod in 1899, when the Lower House suggested a change in the service of confirmation to accommodate adults who had no godparents or who were to be received from other denominations (another request for revision of an existing service in the received book), the episcopate again declined to act, saying that individual bishops could vary the question to suit the occasion.

At most then, the bishops were willing to consider the addition of some necessary material to the Prayer Book in a distinct section. A group of priests and laymen in the Lower

---

1. W.J. Armitage, The Story of the Canadian Revision of the Prayer Book (*Toronto, 1922*) p.2.

2. The General Synod of the Church of England in the Dominion of Canada: Journal of Proceedings of the Second Session, 1896 (*Kingston, 1897*) p.148 (*hereafter referred to as General Synod, Journal of Proceedings with appropriate date*). *General Synod, like Parliament, was made up of two houses. The Upper House consisted of the bishops. The Lower House contained representatives of priests and laity elected from diocesan synods.*

House continued to favour revision, but for the moment they were stopped, as was the work of the Joint Committee, which was, apparently, not directed to undertake any actual revision; and so, nothing was done.

When General Synod assembled again in 1902, however, the issue of revision arose once more. The occasion was a second memorial from the Diocese of Huron asking General Synod to "prepare and authorize" a shortened form of Morning and Evening Prayer for use in school-houses and mission stations. This time, the Lower House was prepared. They did not refer the matter to the Joint Committee on Doctrine, Worship, and Discipline, but moved instead to deal with it themselves.

In a notice of motion printed in the convening circular, J.A. Worrell, K.C., of Toronto, had proposed that a joint committee of both Houses be appointed to "publish an edition of the *Book of Common Prayer* with such additions and adaptations as may be required by the needs of the country."[1] When this motion came before the Lower House, Matthew Wilson, seconded by the Rev. J.C. Farthing (later Bishop of Montreal and long-standing member of revision committees), proposed an amendment calling for a Prayer Book containing "all the Prayers and Forms of Service applicable to and authorized for the use of Church Services in Canada."[2] According to the amendment, the Upper House was to prepare a plan for the issue of the book, and a joint committee would assist in carrying out the plan. This amendment was carefully worded and seemed to place the initiative entirely in the hands of the episcopate, but in doing this, it put them in a position of having to exercise that initiative, and to exercise it in the production of a revision whose authority, furthermore, would derive from the Canadian church.

In an attempt to retreat from the brink, an amendment to the amendment was put, which would follow the same plan of action as the amended motion but group any new material together in an Appendix.[3] The attempt failed, however, and the

---

1. *General Synod*, Journal of Proceedings 1902, *p.110*.
2. *Ibid. p.48.*
3. *Ibid. p.48.*

amended motion carried. The next step was to gain the approval of the Upper House.

A message was sent advising the bishops of the Lower House's action. But the bishops, who had from the first opposed outright revision, while saying they concurred with the action of the Lower House, replied as though asked for an appendix rather than an "edition of the *Book of Common Prayer.*" They agreed to act provided that any services drawn up be sent first to the Provincial Synods, after which, if they received approval, such services could be published in an appendix to the Prayer Book.[1] Faced thus with accepting half a loaf or none, the Lower House concurred, and a Joint Committee on an Appendix to the Prayer Book was formed to prepare material and report to the next General Synod in 1905.

Thus the first step was taken, a hard-won compromise between the Lower House and the diffident conservative bishops. The long venture in self-expression was begun.

Before embarking on that saga, however, it is worth noting that the bishops in 1902 were not simply being obdurate about revision. The desire for a new Prayer Book arose in a much larger context than liturgical revision, as the original notices of motion by Worrell and Wilson make clear. In addition to party loyalties and the fears produced by the ritual battles, other interests too were at work. They bespeak a group of people who envisioned an autonomous church planted in a new land and adapting its expression of the faith to the needs of the growing society. In Worrell's notice of motion, the first business of a proposed joint committee was to give the Church of England in Canada "a distinctive national name." Similarly, Matthew Wilson, in notices of motion four to ten inclusive, called for "a Canadian Prayer Book," modification of the Colonial Clergy Act (37–38 Victoria, Ch.77) so as to give more status to Canadian clergy in England, clarification of the role of the Supreme Court of Canada as final arbiter of ecclesiastical disputes, and other measures designed to establish an Anglican Church of Canada.[2]

1. *Ibid. p.69.*
2. *Ibid. pp.110-112.*

The vision was indeed, as Baldwin had said of Wilson's first proposal six years earlier, "venturesome"; but this was the age of Laurier and Sifton, the wheat boom, the first Canadian stock and bond market, and exuberant railway land schemes. The Prime Minister had said the twentieth century belonged to Canada, and from 1890 to 1910 this indeed seemed to be true. As the band played and growing numbers jumped on its wagon, men with the church's best interests at heart thought that it too should join the nationalist parade. But the Upper House and a minority of the Lower House saw things differently. Perhaps it was just the old Tory instinct, or the belief that the church had other and more pressing demands on its time and attention. Whatever the reason, the effort at nationalizing the church, for the time being, came to nothing. But at least it gave tongue to a point of view little heard since the early days of George Mountain and John Strachan: the Canadian church was not simply the Church of England in Canada.

The Appendix
The problem of the conservatism of the bishops had been overcome in this case by compromise, but the attempt at implementing the agreement reached brought into play all the other obstacles: geographical distances, financial limitations, and party strife. A century later, the difficulties created by these are still worth considering.

The Joint Committee charged with preparing the appendix was chaired by H.T. Kingdon, Bishop of Fredericton, who within the first year called the members together in Montreal. Very few, however, attended this meeting; in fact, it is unlikely that the whole Committee ever met. Those who did attend at Montreal appointed Kingdon (along with Bishops Baldwin of Huron, Hamilton of Ottawa, and Pinkham of Calgary) as a subcommittee whose task was to draw up the appendix; and at the insistence of the others, the chairman himself was to "undertake the work at once and hasten it on as much as possible."[1]

1. H.T. Kingdon, as quoted in Armitage, op. cit., p.10.

Bishop H.T. Kingdon of Fredericton was chairman of the General Synod Committee charged with preparing a Canadian appendix to the 1662 Prayer Book. He and Francis Partridge, Dean of his cathedral, were left to do the work themselves.

Left thus to his own devices, Kingdon began work, assisted by Francis Partridge, dean of his cathedral. Partridge, apparently, had been the only member of the Lower House present at Montreal; and since the Lower House had originated the business; it seemed logical, said Kingdon, to seek his advice.

As disconcerting as the indifference of his Committee may have been, Kingdon was soon to realize that this was not the only problem he faced. To begin with, since the tremendous distances separating the Committee members and the cost of travel relative to the church's finances made meeting together a virtual impossibility, Kingdon resorted to using the mail to circulate his proposals and solicit responses to them.[1] Unfortunately, however, as Wilson wrote to Kingdon, approval by mail from separate individuals was not the same as approval after discussion by a committee meeting together.[2]

Another difficulty arose from party strife in the Canadian church and the personal enmities aroused thereby. The four bishops on the subcommittee seem to have been chosen with a

---

1. Apart from Kingdon and Partridge, the only other Maritimers on the Committee were Archdeacon Neales of Woodstock, N.S., and Justice Ritchie of Halifax. Bishop Hunter Dunn, two clergy and two laity were from Quebec. Four bishops, three priests and two laymen were from Ontario, and one bishop and three priests from the west. Kingdon was correct about the impossibility of holding meetings. The distances and cost of travel were critical here and would be in the future in the work of producing the revision of 1918.

2. M. Wilson, quoted in Armitage, op. cit., p.9.

view to constituting a broadly representative group,[1] and this stratagem might have succeeded if they had met and worked together. However, working separately through the mail only engendered suspicions and enhanced already extant prejudices. When, for example, Kingdon, a well-accredited heir of the catholic revival in England, attempted to circulate a first draft of the appendix for comment by other members of the subcommittee, it went first to Baldwin, a staunch Low Churchman, and then disappeared. Kingdon's ascerbic comment to Wilson on the disappearance was that he supposed his manuscript had "lighted some fires in London."[2]

Kingdon next sent a second draft to each of the three other bishops, and although there was no reply from Baldwin, Hamilton and Pinkham both approved the proposal. As a result the work was published in pamphlet form and, being circulated to all the members of the Joint Committee, gained approval by the majority. A copy of this original appendix (no longer extant) was seen by Ramsay Armitage, who said it came to over 260 pages and noted its contents.

The appendix proposed by Kingdon gained the approval of a majority of the Committee members, but the "vote" was by no means unanimous. Wilson, for one, complained that it went far beyond what he had wanted,[3] and subsequent events indicate that others felt the same way. The details of what followed are obscure, but the original appendix was never presented to the General Synod. The Primate, Archbishop Bond, had the material "examined on behalf of the Synod, by one well fitted for the duty;"[4] as a result, the work was reduced to less than a quarter its original size and, in Armitage's words, "almost everywhere, shows a free use of the knife."[5]

When this truncated version was presented to the Lower House at the General Synod of 1905 in Quebec City, there

---

1. Cf. Charles H. Mockridge, The Bishops of the Church of England in Canada and Newfoundland (Toronto, 1896) pp.326, 334, 351, & 356.
2. Kingdon to Wilson, quoted in Armitage, op. cit., p.10.
3. Armitage, op. cit., p.9.
4. Ibid. p.18.
5. Ibid. p.17.

were, as Armitage puts it, "many enemies who stood ready to kill it and bury it beyond recall."[1] The motion to receive the report was amended to send the appendix back to the Committee, where further suggestions could be considered and the result printed and distributed to members prior to the next General Synod. Despite impassioned and articulate opposition, this amendment eventually passed by a large majority, an apparent victory for High Churchmen and those favouring adaptation of the Prayer Book to Canadian needs. During the hours of debate on this issue, however, irreparable damage had been done, and Armitage attributes this primarily to Dyson Hague who, as he says, "gave the Appendix its quietus."[2]

Hague was the rector of St. Paul's Church, Halifax, a stronghold of the militantly Low Church Colonial and Continental Church Society. He was an intelligent, informed, and convinced Low Churchman who saw clearly what the issue was and stated his party's position eloquently in his book, *The Protestantism of the Prayer Book*.

The two key doctrines of the catholic revival in the church were, said Hague, sacramental grace and the sacrifice of the mass.[3] The Tractarian appeal to the Prayer Book of 1549 in support of these key doctrines he rejected, because that book had been rejected, just as were, for example, the Six Articles of Henry VIII. Hague based his own position on the contention that "omission and alteration are practical prohibition" and that the Prayer Book was "the product of certain men, and of a certain age, and must be interpreted in the light of that age, and in honest accordance with the known view of its compilers."[4]

Accordingly, Hague considered Morning Prayer, Evening Prayer, and the Litany to be "the main body of the liturgy" and well able to stand "vigorous scrutiny" regarding their Protestant orthodoxy. He included the eucharist with the "occa-

1. *Ibid. p.11.*
2. *Kingdon to Wilson, quoted in Armitage, op. cit., p.11.*
3. *Dyson Hague,* The Protestantism of the Prayer Book *(Toronto, 1890) p.XV.*
4. *Ibid. p.XVI.*

sional services" such as baptism and ordination, but felt it too would pass the test.[1] The central idea of the Church of England communion service, Hague believed, was to remember Christ's meritorious cross and passion, by faith in which our sins are remitted and we are made partakers of the Kingdom of Heaven.

> Solemnity, simplicity, practical fitness, all are wonderfully and thoroughly combined [in the 1662 Eucharist]. The exhortations, so heart-rending and real; the confession, so fitted to the contrite heart; the absolution and the sentences, so full of consolation; the following prayers, so scriptural and pure; the Lord's prayer, and thanksgiving, so natural and significant; and the final ascription of praise to God — what could be more edifying and precious? To the devout soul everything combines to bring one into the very presence of God, to see the Saviour face to face, and to feed upon Him in the heart, by faith, with thanksgiving.[2]

In Hague's description of the eucharist, nothing could speak more articulately for the Low Church point of view than his dismissal of the whole Canon in one short phrase: "the following prayers." He saw the whole Tractarian movement as "cleverly disguised" Romanism, and advised his readers that "as long as the *Book of Common Prayer* remains unchanged, the Church can never be Romanized."[3]

In a concluding passage, which perhaps foreshadowed his words in the debate on the appendix, Hague exhorts that

> considering the state of the Church as a whole it seems to me that it is the wisdom of Protestant Churchmen to be content with the Prayer Book they have, and in the shape they have it.... And it is certain that were any revision attempted, the tendency at present would be to introduce changes of a retrograde charac-

---

1. *Ibid. pp.41-42.*
2. *Ibid. p. 53. Cf. Gregory Dix, The Shape of the Liturgy (Westminster, 1945) p. 671 f. and E.C. Ratcliff, The Communion Service of the Prayer Book, Chichester Diocesan Gazette, Vol. XVI (1935) pp. 7-12, quoted in Tripp, David H. and E.C. Ratcliff: Reflections on Liturgical Revision (Bramcote Notts: Grove Books, 1980).*
3. *Ibid. (Dyson Hague) p.XIII.*

The Rev. Dyson Hague, then rector of St. Paul's Church, Halifax, is credited with bringing about the rejection of the Appendix to the Prayer Book by General Synod in 1905. Hague was an intelligent and articulate apologist for the Protestant aspect of Anglicanism. He opposed High Anglican doctrine on principle, and perhaps shared a suspicion of Kingdon whose brother in England had become Roman Catholic.

ter ... the tide is set on the current of High Anglican doctrine ... in the event of any attempted authoritative revision of the Prayer Book, changes might be made that would ... restore the word "altar" ... employ the word "sacrifice" ... expunge the post-Communion rubric [the black rubric] ... exchange the long-disused and doubtfully legal Ornaments rubric for a law binding all the clergy. They would, in fact ... assimilate the Prayer Book ... to the Prayer Book of the Scottish Episcopal Church; nay, the great majority ... would be satisfied with nothing less than a return to the First Prayer Book of Edward VI....[1]

He concludes by quoting from the *Church Review* the intention on the part of English catholics of restoring the mass to "its seat of honour as the sun and centre of Christian worship" and warns "the risk of change is fearfully great."[2]

All this notwithstanding, however, by a vote of more than two to one, the Lower House had expressed its approval of an appendix and its support for the Committee, which was now to prepare a second draft in the light of suggestions forwarded to it, to be distributed prior to the next General Synod. Accordingly, a message was sent informing the Upper House of this decision, and in due course a message from the bishops returned. However, this episcopal message reflected not the tally of the votes, but the heat of the argument that had preceded the vote in the Lower House; the Upper House regretted it

1. *Ibid.* pp.141-143.
2. *Ibid.* p.144.

could not concur in referring the appendix back to the Committee and was of the opinion, moreover, that the best interest of the church would be "conserved and promoted by deferring the consideration of the whole subject."[1]

In the Lower House there was indignation. They voted against concurring with the bishops, set up a committee to confer with the Upper House about their non-concurrence, and sent back a message asking their Lordships to be pleased to receive this deputation. At the subsequent meeting the committee reported the "very strong desire" of the Lower House to continue work on the appendix. They reminded the bishops of the numerous memorials[2] requesting either an appendix or a revision, and stated their opinion that the response of the Upper House gave "a permanent quietus to the whole matter," which in light of the memorials and the vote in the Lower House, they could scarce justify to their constituents.[3] The bishops acknowledged the truth of all this and promised to reconsider, but in the end could only re-affirm their original decision "on account of the divergence of opinion which at present prevails on the subject."[4] With "regrets" the Lower House acknowledged acceptance.

So the first attempt of the Canadian Church to alter the  Prayer Book came to nothing, defeated by doctrinal disagreement and the strength of party antipathies.[5] Ironically,

---

1. *General Synod,* Journal of Proceedings 1905, p.57.
2. *Ibid.* pp.123-126.
3. *Ibid.* p.62.
4. *Ibid.* p.63.
5. *It is difficult today to realize the intensity of party rivalries or the irrational fears they still aroused in the early years of this century. Some appreciation for the view from the Upper House of General Synod may be obtained from a novel,* The Priest, *which went through seven editions between 1906 and 1909. The book is about the Secret Society of Nicodemus whose purpose was "banishing forever from the Church of England the bastard faith of Protestantism" and the covert conversion of that body from within to Rome. The leader of this group is Father Severn, "a huge and burley man... of full and striking face, which was bronzed and greasy.... His shoulders were high, his neck short, his ribs wide, and his arms of unnatural length. His skeleton resembled that of an anthropomorphous ape...." The members are characterized as "little minded men content to practise slyness and treachery for the gratification which such conspiracy brought to their senses... men who were Romanists for the love of coloured vestments, elaborate ritual and*

Kingdon, who chaired the Appendix Committee and did most of the work, probably accepted the outcome with some satisfaction. As he had said to Wilson two years earlier, he would personally have preferred to let each bishop issue such services and prayers as were necessary for his own diocese, and then through usage and adaptation allow a gradual agreement to come forth on what was best for the church as a whole.[1]

(Note 5, continued from page 33) all the more childish and effeminate aspects of religion...." The Society is extensively funded by the influential Bishop of Warborough, who joined it as a foolish youth and is now being blackmailed with threats to his only and beloved son. And lest any of this should be dismissed as sensationalism founded on Protestant nightmares, the author, in a preface to the Popular Edition, upheld the existence of such a society and insisted the main outlines of his story were hard fact which persons openly identified elsewhere did not dare refute. Cf. Harold Begbie, The Priest (London, 1906).

1. Armitage, op. cit., p.10. Kingdon was far ahead of his contemporaries in conceiving of liturgy as a dynamic thing evolving in response to the circumstances and perceptions of its participants.

5

Revision begun: The establishment of principles and practice

T he issue so firmly consigned to limbo did not long remain there. The very next General Synod launched the church on the path of full revision, a decision made possible by the dissipation of the previous obstacles: the Upper House's uncertainty about whether the process would get out of hand, the problems inherent in the size of the country, and the fear of Low Churchmen that revision would separate them from their historical base as a valid expression of the faith of the English church.

The first obstacle was overcome by a concerted initiative of all the bishops of the Anglican Communion. At the Lambeth Conference in the summer of 1908,[1] Prayer Book revision was made one of the chief concerns. It was agreed that "adaptation and enrichment of forms of service and worship" is advisable and even essential in order for the church to meet the needs of people who are of different races and who live in different parts of the world.[2] This agreement in principle was given more specific expression in two Resolutions. Resolution number 27 recommended the adaptation of rubrics to generally accepted custom; the streamlining of services by the omission of repetitious or redundant elements; the framing of additions designed to enrich present services; provision of alternative forms of service and greater "elasticity" in their use; replacement of words whose intended meaning had become ob-

---

1. Almost two years after the royal warrant of November 10, 1906, had opened the way for revision in the Church of England.
2. Encyclical Letter. Conference of Bishops of the Anglican Communion: Holden at Lambeth Palace July 6 to August 5, 1908 (London, 1908) p.35 (hereafter referred to as The Lambeth Conference Report).

scure; and review of the calendar and tables prefixed to the book. Resolution number 28 suggested that the Archbishop of Canterbury and other bishops prepare a sort of catalogue of special forms of service, which could then be selectively implemented by various bishops as needed in their dioceses.[1]

Canadian bishops returning home in August to prepare for a General Synod in a month's time, when revision might be expected to be urged again, now possessed accepted guidelines within which orderly change could be undertaken. They may also have been given other incentives to proceed. In his charge to the General Synod of 1915, at which a revised book was approved in essence, Archbishop Matheson would speak of the urging by some English bishops that the Canadian church, unfettered by civil law, "should lead in the issue of such a safe and wise revision of the Prayer Book as will show that the Book can be revised and enriched and yet remain in its essential and precious features the same Book."[2]

Such an "understanding" may have played a part in overcoming the obstacles of distance and cost too, since the Cambridge University Press agreed to underwrite the cost of producing the revision in return for the book's copyright.

And finally, as to Low Church fears that any departure from 1662 would weaken their position, while it was true that the implementation of Resolution 27 would indeed involve revision, the effect of Resolution 28 would only be to allow a sort of appendix to exist as a local variant in some dioceses. It would have no authority beyond the diocese, and hence, it would leave the 1662 Prayer Book intact as the sole repository of the national church's faith and order. Thus, as the General Synod approached, Hague, accepting the inevitability of some change, prepared a notice of motion that "no Canadian edition of the *Book of Common Prayer* be issued for the present," but rather that "the Bishops be requested to publish instead ... the special services authorized for use in the various Dioceses for Thanksgiving, Missions, Laying of Foundation Stones,

---

1. *Ibid. p.52f. Resolutions Number 27 & 28.*
2. *General Synod,* Journal of Proceedings 1915, *p.15.*

Consecration of Churches, etc. together with a list of the permissible adaptations and modifications which they have already conditionally authorized."[1] The Canadian church could still take the lead in revision, but in the minimalist fashion of Resolution 28, which would please Low Churchmen both in Canada and England.

When the synod met, however, it had before it not only Hague's motion but one by J.C. Farthing calling for revisions,[2] and also the expected memorial from the Diocese of Huron, urging continued effort to produce a Canadian edition of the Prayer Book.[3] In view of the action by Lambeth, these proposals now took on added appeal. Furthermore, the General Synod had just completed a new hymnal which was highly praised by the primate, and delegates soon concluded that they were surely capable of revising the Prayer Book as well.[4]

The outcome was a motion by the Lower House, concurred in by the Upper House, that all recommendations relating to enrichment and adaptation of the Prayer Book be referred to a special Joint Committee to consider and report on at the next synod, the only restriction being to keep within the guidelines laid down by Lambeth.[5] That committee was the Joint Committee on the Enrichment and Adaptation of the *Book of Common Prayer* (commonly called the General Committee).

Thus, with the obstacles to revision overcome, work could now proceed. But the motion of General Synod which produced the General Committee was phrased in terms which left a great deal to be interpreted, and so the first business was to decide about matters of organization and procedure. The structure and system of working which took shape is worth noting in some detail for several reasons. In the first place, it was effective. Also, it was adopted again for the second revision. It

---

1. *General Synod of the Church of England in the Dominion of Canada*, Convening Circular for the Fifth Session, 1908, *p.6f.*
2. Convening Circular for the Fifth Session, *1908, p.9.*
3. *General Synod*, Journal of Proceedings 1908, *p.164.*
4. *Armitage, op. cit., p.23.*
5. *General Synod*, Journal of Proceedings 1908, *p.132.*

focused the old party disagreement — the still unsettled question from the Reformation of how Christians were to work out their salvation. And finally, it forced Anglicans once again to put unity and the practice of the faith ahead of theological considerations.[1]

The first suggestion was that the Committee simply "receive, consider and tabulate" suggestions. This would have accomplished little and thrown the question of revision back to General Synod. Bishop Davidson of Montreal would have made the Committee's role an active one, that of taking the necessary steps to get suggestions. Again, however, it was Huron Diocese which got the project moving. Bishop Williams, in an early display of the energy and determination which was to win him fame (or notoriety[2]) amongst Committee members, moved that "a subcommittee[3] be approved to draft such suggestions and additions to the Prayer Book as may seem advisable in order to meet the needs of the Church."[4] This motion passed by a vote of nine to five. The Committee (the subcommittee) was to report to the General Committee (the Central Revision Committee), which in turn would report to General Synod.

Thus, a recommendation would have to pass three scrutinies, each at a broader level, before gaining acceptance. But it was the Committee which undertook the major task of establishing the basic criteria by which suggestions would receive consideration at all. The establishment of these criteria occu-

---

1. Cf. above, p. 14.
2. Armitage, op. cit., p.74.
3. This subcommittee became the Central Revision Subcommittee which carried out the bulk of the work. It will henceforth be referred to as the Committee. Other subcommittees will be referred to by their particular name, and the Joint Committee on the Enrichment and Adaptation of the Book of Common Prayer will be referred to as the General Committee.
4. Minutes of the Joint Committee of the General Synod of Canada on the Enrichment and Adaptation of the Book of Common Prayer, the meeting of January 7, 1909, attached to the Minute Book of the Committee of General Synod of the Church of England in Canada for the Adaptation, Enrichment and Revision of the Book of Common Prayer. Revision of 1915-1918, now in the Archives of the Anglican Church of Canada, Toronto (hereafter referred to as the General Committee Minutes).

pied a great deal of time at all three levels. Their establish-ment, however, was crucial to the future direction of revision, since these criteria, by determining the type and extent of ma-terial to be considered, would also determine the degree of in-fluence on the final product of that perception of the faith em-bodied in each of the rival parties in the church.

The initial engagement between these rivals took place at the Committee's first meeting on 20 April 1909. The High Church party moved that General Synod publish a Canadian edition of the Prayer Book with additional services and more permissive rubrics. But the motion stipulated, as the criterion for inclusion, that "no change shall be made in Doctrine, Dis-cipline or Sacraments as put forth in the present Prayer Book."[1] The key reference here was to "Doctrine, Discipline or Sacraments," a paraphrase of the wording of the Solemn Dec-laration of 1893: "And we are determined by the help of God to hold and maintain the Doctrine, Sacraments and Discipline of Christ."[2] The Declaration declared the church in Canada to be "in full communion with the Church of England through-out the world." Thus, if allusion to the Solemn Declaration was to be allowed, it could bring in as referents not only the 1549-type canon of the Scottish church and the American church but indeed, the whole Tractarian theology and, per-haps, the Ritualist movement which sprang from it.

A Low Church amendment stipulated "no addition or change ... which would in any way make or indicate a change in doctrines or principles of the Church of England in Canada."[3] This tied revision firmly to 1662; in fact, it bound it. All might agree to reject any suggestions which made a change in doctrine or principle, but the essential point of this amend-ment was that nothing be allowed which might even "indi-cate" such a change. Thus, for example, there could be no clarification of matters that had become confused to the ad-

---

1. *Minutes of the Sub-Committee of the Committee of General Synod on Adap-tation and Enrichment of the Prayer Book. Meeting of April 20, 1909. Now in the Archives of the Anglican Church of Canada, Toronto.*
2. Book of Common Prayer, Canada, 1962, p.VIII.
3. *Minutes of the Sub-Committee, April 20, 1909.*

vantage of Low Churchmen: that the eucharist was not an occasional office like baptism or marriage, despite its position in
the Prayer Book, or that the ornaments rubric, at the very
least, did envisage some ornaments. And thus, for example, at
the General Synod of 1915, as a result of that added limitation,
the provision of propers for use at a nuptial mass would be
ruled out of order on the grounds that it would imply a change
of principle and therefore exceed the mandate of the General
Committee (the word *indicate* had been changed to "imply").[1]

But in 1909, as the first meeting of the Committee seemed
to be ready to favour the Low Church amendment, the High
Churchmen came back with an amendment to the amendment, requiring that a statement be added to the amendment
that no change be made which would in any way contradict
the Solemn Declaration. This second amendment betrayed
the tone of those who, expecting defeat, strove to preserve at
least a minimum; but even this failed. The proposal of an
amendment to the amendment forced a vote in which the
original motion lost decisively and the amendment won.[2]

Armitage notes that the adoption of this measure was important, because it would be eventually adopted by General
Synod and would furnish "the principle upon which the whole
work of revision was undertaken and carried to a successful
conclusion."[3] This was, in fact, a turning point in the struggle
between the Low and High Church factions. From the early
days of the church in Canada when Inglis had spoken out
against them as "Congregationalists," there had been a large
and influential group of churchmen in whom democratic principles, the isolation of frontier life, and personal conviction
had combined to produce a solid Low Church constituency,
often of Calvinist or Zwinglian theology. They had always,
however, been the weaker of the two groups in the Canadian
church, depending on local pockets of power in a generally
old-High Church establishment. They stood to lose in a gen-

---

1. *General Synod*, Journal of Proceedings 1915, *p.64f.*
2. *Minutes of the Sub-Committee*, April 20, 1909.
3. *Armitage, op. cit., p.27.*

eral assembly and had thus successively opposed diocesan, provincial, and national synods. The first General Synod of 1893 had been a triumph for the High Church party, not only in its coming to pass, but also because, through it, High Church views of what the church intended itself to be had been entrenched in the Solemn Declaration.

At this point in time, however, the High Church position in Canada had for some time been in decline. Secessions to Rome in England and a large Roman Catholic population at home had created, among churchmen generally, a distrust of the High Church, with the result that this group had seen its lay foundation eroded and had become increasingly a clerical party. By contrast, Low Churchmen, at first afraid of the power of a General Synod, had in 1905 discovered their own power in that body: strong clerical leaders, assured of lay support, were able to exert an influence disproportionate to their numbers, because they could sway the Upper House.[1]

In any case, now at the Committee stage, by a vote of nine to seven, the Low Church had secured themselves, liturgically at least, from the implications of the Solemn Declaration.

The struggle continued when, two years later, the Committee's report was presented to the General Committee and the motion came up again for approval. This time, evidently, things were less decorous, and after a time Bishop Williams tried unsuccessfully to get a twenty-minute adjournment during which tempers could cool and informal discussion take place. In desperation, the High Church members tried to amend the Committee's motion to say that the 1662 book would be untouched and any changes would be printed at the end: an appendix (the refuge of the underdog, since being separate it could be ignored or have its authority slighted), was grasped at again, this time by the High Church Party. Argument continued with procedural moves and counter-moves and, finally, to cap the confusion, a second motion (passed while the first was still on the floor) allowed two clergy who were not members of the Committee to enter the room. Who

---

1. Cf. above, p.29-32.

they were and what they did is not recorded, but their effect was momentous. The motion on revision was proposed and passed unanimously, as was a second motion that all changes would be consistent with Resolution 27 of the Lambeth Conference of 1908.[1]

It may be assumed that the two mysterious entrants argued for the necessity of presenting a common front. The animosity between High and Low factions had scuttled the last attempt at change in 1905, and undoubtedly the bishops would not hesitate to intervene again if it seemed that revision was likely to revive the dreadful battles of the late nineteenth century. Certainly, when the time came, great care was taken in presenting the report to General Synod in 1911, to portray revision as the desired goal of the whole church. The memorials of 1905 were "interpreted" to show a desire for revision, and the struggles over wording of the main motion were presented as "divergences of opinion" concerning the power of General Synod to revise the Prayer Book and with respect to the exact duties of the Committees.[2]

As for the motion itself, it was broken into three motions, each one made by Canon Cody and seconded by Dean Crawford, representatives, Armitage notes, of "the two great schools of thought in the Church."[3] The first asked for a Joint Committee "to prepare or compile" enrichments and make provision for necessary adaptations; the second promised that no change in text or rubric would "involve or imply a change of doctrine or of fundamental principles, it being always understood that the ornaments rubric be left untouched"; and the third provided for revisions to be inserted in the body of the book.[4]

These motions passed easily with, however, one small but significant change to the second proposal made in an amendment by Dr. J.A. Worrell, Chancellor of Toronto, and the ubiquitous Matthew Wilson. The change was to remove the

---

1. *Minutes of the Joint Committee*, April 26, 1911.
2. *General Synod*, Journal of Proceedings 1911, *p.240 f.*
3. *Armitage, op. cit., p.40.*
4. *Ibid. p.40.*

word *fundamental* from the provision that there would be no change which would "involve or imply a change of doctrine or of fundamental principles."[1] With the word *fundamental* removed, Armitage notes, this provision "strengthened the safeguards proposed ... it became what might be called a saving clause in the work of revision, which prevented action along doubtful lines."[2] "There were at times," he notes elsewhere, "subjects for discussion which touched the very depth of conviction, and division would be clearly marked, but the charter under which we were working prevented any departure from the principles of the *Book of Common Prayer.*"[3] It "ruled out of practical politics a large number of debatable questions which otherwise would have caused many difficulties. This proved to be especially true in regard to the Holy Communion."[4]

Thus, a strong clearly defined framework was set up which allowed revision to proceed and prevented party differences (which would seriously disrupt the life of the church) from entering into the process. The situation was summarized in the report of the General Committee to the General Synod of 1915. It began by noting the ambivalence of the church's attitude toward revision: "Attempts to deal with Prayer Book Revision for the past eighteen years in General Synod are evidence of a desire to render the *Book of Common Prayer* more serviceable.... At the same time deep anxiety was felt lest any attempt to touch the Prayer Book might lead to such radical revision as to destroy the balance of the concordat which it represents or mar the beauty of its ideal of worship." The instructions outlining the scope of the work were "a most valuable aid to the Committee, for by them a whole mass of proposals, some of far-reaching effect, some more or less academic,

---

1. *General Synod,* Journal of Proceedings 1911, *p.41 f.*
2. *Armitage, op. cit., p.41.*
3. *Ibid. p.72.*
4. *Ibid. p.245.*

THE COMMUNION.

ous Name; evermore praising thee, and saying, Holy, holy, holy, Lord God of hosts, heaven and earth are full of thy glory: Glory be to thee, O Lord most High. *Amen.*

PROPER PREFACES.

Upon Christmas-day, and seven days after.

BECAUSE thou didst give Jesus Christ thine only Son to be born as at this time for us; who, by the operation of the Holy Ghost, was made very man of the substance of the Virgin Mary his mother; and that without spot of sin, to make us clean from all sin. Therefore with Angels, &c.

Upon Easter-day, and seven days after.

BUT chiefly are we bound to praise thee for the glorious Resurrection of thy Son Jesus Christ our Lord: for he is the very Paschal Lamb, which was offered for us, and hath taken away the sin of the world; who by his death hath destroyed death, and by his rising to life again hath restored to us everlasting life. Therefore with Angels, &c.

Upon Ascension-day, and seven days after.

THROUGH thy most dearly beloved Son Jesus Christ our Lord; who after his most glorious Resurrection manifestly appeared to all his Apostles, and in their sight ascended up into heaven to prepare a place for us; that where he is, thither we might also ascend, and reign with him in glory. Therefore with Angels, &c.

Upon Whit-sunday, and six days after.

THROUGH Jesus Christ our Lord; according to whose most true promise, the Holy Ghost came down as at this time from heaven with a sudden great sound, as it had been a mighty wind, in the likeness of fiery tongues, lighting upon the Apostles, to teach them, and to lead them to all truth; giving them both the gift of divers languages, and also boldness with fervent zeal constantly to preach the Gospel unto all nations; whereby we have been brought out of darkness and error into the clear light and true knowledge of thee,

The 1662 Communion Service was left unchanged in the 1918 book. It is interesting to notice here the place of the Prayer of Humble Access between the Sanctus and the Prayer of Consecration. The absence of page numbers would bewilder modern Anglicans.

THE COMMUNION.

and of thy Son Jesus Christ. Therefore with Angels, &c.

Upon the Feast of Trinity only.

WHO art one God, one Lord ; not one only Person, but three Persons in one Substance. For that which we believe of the glory of the Father, the same we believe of the Son, and of the Holy Ghost, without any difference or inequality. Therefore with Angels, &c.

¶ *After each of which Prefaces shall immediately be sung or said,*

THEREFORE with Angels and Archangels, and with all the company of heaven, we laud and magnify thy glorious Name ; evermore praising thee, and saying, Holy, holy, holy, Lord God of hosts, heaven and earth are full of thy glory: Glory be to thee, O Lord most High. *Amen.*

¶ *Then shall the Priest, kneeling down at the Lord's Table, say in the name of all them that shall receive the Communion this Prayer following.*

WE do not presume to come to this thy Table, O merciful Lord, trusting in our own righteousness, but in thy manifold and great mercies. We are not worthy so much as to gather up the crumbs under thy Table. But thou art the same Lord, whose property is always to have mercy : Grant us therefore, gracious Lord, so to eat the flesh of thy dear Son Jesus Christ, and to drink his blood, that our sinful bodies may be made clean by his body, and our souls washed through his most precious blood, and that we may evermore dwell in him, and he in us. *Amen.*

¶ *When the Priest, standing before the Table, hath so ordered the Bread and Wine, that he may with the more readiness and decency break the Bread before the people, and take the Cup into his hands, he shall say the Prayer of Consecration, as followeth.*

ALMIGHTY God, our heavenly Father, who of thy tender mercy didst give thine only Son Jesus Christ to suffer death upon the cross for our redemption ; who made there (by his one oblation of himself once offered) a full, perfect, and sufficient sacrifice, oblation, and satisfaction, for the sins of the whole world ; and did institute, and in his holy Gospel command us to continue, a perpetual memory of that his precious

Notice the rubric in the middle of the right hand column. Here, in 1662, for the first time, this previously unnamed prayer is designated as "the Prayer of Consecration." The term means to set apart or make something holy. It was first used in reference to the bread and wine by John Pearson (1613-86), Lady Margaret professor of divinity at Cambridge and, later, Bishop of Chester.

were swept aside,"[1] and furthermore, they made it possible to complete the work and to do so in the time prescribed.

In sum, then, the purpose was to effect "a *minimum*, not a *maximum*, change, even in the appearance of the Book,"[2] and in the words of Archbishop Matheson, this resulted in "a sane and conservative revision."[3]

The struggle to establish parameters for the work of revision tells us a lot about the church in the first part of the twentieth century. The makeup and function of the revising body and its constituent parts speaks volumes about its self-concept.

The General Committee was elected from the membership of General Synod and consisted of 20 bishops, 25 priests, and 15 laymen under the chairmanship of the primate. It functioned as a supervisory body, reviewing all things submitted to it, and reporting to General Synod. In order to win approval in the General Committee, any proposed changes in the Prayer Book had to be approved by a two-thirds majority.

The General Committee did its work by creating a number of subcommittees: one on the lectionary and calendar, others on the use of the psalter, special services, and business. The most important of these subcommittees was the Central Revision Subcommittee (the Committee), to which all the other subcommittees were directly responsible and which itself took responsibility for all work on the daily offices, the eucharist, and the occasional offices. It reported "from time to time" to the General Committee.

The membership of the subcommittees was arrived at by electing a nominating committee from among the General Committee. The nominating committee then presented its choices to the General Committee. In the case of the Central Revision Subcommittee, its choices were accepted unchanged, but with two names added from the floor. It had 26 members in

1. Report of the Secretary of the Joint Committee of Both Houses on the Adaptation, Enrichment and Revision of the Book of Common Prayer *with Resolutions Prepared in Due Form Covering All the Adaptations, Enrichments and Revisions Proposed by the Committee (London, 1914) p.7f.*
2. *Ibid. p.8.*
3. *Minutes of the Central Revision Sub-Committee, April 28, 1912.1. General Synod,* Journal of Proceedings, *1915, p.16*

all: the primate was a member ex-officio, Bishop Williams of Huron was chairman, and Archdeacon Armitage, the secretary.

Within the Central Revision Subcommittee the procedure was equable and efficient. Any 12 members constituted a quorum as long as all three orders were represented.[1] Any motion proposing changes in the Prayer Book needed a two-thirds majority of those present to be accepted on a first-draft basis. If, after discussion, amendments were proposed, these could be approved by a simple majority. After each meeting, the minutes were to be printed and circulated to all members. At the next meeting, changes previously initiated had to be confirmed by a simple majority or rejected entirely, no further amendment of them could be made.[2]

The basic structure of the revising body was therefore a four-tiered hierarchy made up of General Synod, the Joint Committee of General Synod on the Enrichment, Adaptation, and Revision of the Book of Common Prayer (the General Committee), the Central Revision Subcommittee (the Committee), and the other subcommittees created specifically for one job. The hub of this constellation, however, was the Central Revision Subcommittee, which functioned at the intermediate level for all matters of concern, but also functioned at the most specific level for the essential areas of the daily offices, the eucharist, and the occasional offices. This, and three additional things, made the Central Revision Subcommittee the major influence in revision: it alone dealt with the daily and weekly worship of the church, the heart of the Prayer Book; it functioned as a clearing house and filter for whatever went to the General Committee; and its members (already the most conversant with what was being done) were also members of both the General Committee (which must endorse its work) and of General Synod (the final court of decision). This struc-

---

1. Minutes of the Joint Committee, Sept. 13, 1911, and April 28, 1914. Cf. also General Synod, Journal of Proceedings 1908, p.141, and Minutes of the Joint Committee, January 7, 1909.
2. Minutes of the Central Revision Sub-Committee, April 28, 1912.

ture was adopted again in 1943 for the Prayer Book's second revision.

6

The revision of Morning Prayer and the Holy Eucharist

When the Committe was ready to begin the actual work of revising, one of its first concerns was to regularize Morning Prayer as a service in its own right. During four days devoted to this purpose, in the spring of 1912, a good deal of time was spent in amiable debate about the merits of various proposed additions to the opening Sentences. But the principle task, first voiced in 1851 by the Quebec Conference of Canadian bishops, was the addition of rubrical authorization for a sermon and an offering, by means of which Matins could stand alone as the Sunday morning service.[1] These changes were easily made, but a difficulty still to be faced in achieving this purpose lay with the rubric governing the Creed: "Then shall be sung or said the Apostles' Creed ... except only such days as the Creed of St. Athanasius is appointed to be read."[2] This thorny subject, already a contentious issue by reason of the English debates,[3] was broached at a meeting that fall. It was the beginning of a long and, at times, angry and personal debate which ended in the Athanasian Creed being kept in the book but made optional at Morning Prayer: "Then shall be said or sung the Apostles' Creed, or the Creed of St. Athanasius."[4] This provision got the Athanasian Creed safely out of required use but retained its authority in the Prayer Book. All that re-

---

1. *Minutes of the Central Revision Subcommittee, April 20, 1912.* Cf. The Book of Common Prayer, *Canada, 1918, p.19.*
2. Book of Common Prayer 1662, *Morning Prayer.*
3. *Jasper, op. cit., p.114.*
4. *Minutes of the Central Revision Subcommittee, August 28,1912.* Cf. The Book of Common Prayer, *Canada, 1918, p.13.*

THE BOOK OF
COMMON PRAYER

AND

ADMINISTRATION OF THE SACRAMENTS

AND OTHER RITES AND CEREMONIES OF THE CHURCH
ACCORDING TO THE USE OF

THE CHURCH OF ENGLAND
IN THE DOMINION OF CANADA

TOGETHER WITH

THE PSALTER OR PSALMS OF DAVID

POINTED AS THEY ARE TO BE SUNG OR SAID IN CHURCHES

AND THE FORM OR MANNER OF MAKING
ORDAINING AND CONSECRATING OF
BISHOPS PRIESTS AND DEACONS

CAMBRIDGE
AT THE UNIVERSITY PRESS
TORONTO : 215-219 VICTORIA STREET

Pica

Copyright

The title page of the 1918 Prayer Book makes clear its Canadian identity.

mained was to give rubrical recognition to the separation of the Sunday liturgy into its three component parts.[1] The Low Church now had its "Sunday Morning Service," and the High Church now had the eucharist standing alone;[2] thus both the sacramental and non-sacramental answers to the Reformation question of how persons were to work out their salvation from day to day were set free to make their appeal to Canadian Anglicans. To give formal recognition to things so long and widely practised as to be customary was, seemingly, a modest accomplishment. But it was a clear unequivocal piece of revision, acknowledging the truth of the Anglican situation — that of a church in which the critical question about the means of grace[3] was still unanswered but could continue to linger until a solution might appear which was comprehensive rather than divisive.

The major discussion of the eucharist took place at the Committee's meeting in the spring of 1913, and occupied less than two days. It began with the adoption of the title unchanged as in the 1662 book; the rest of the session is accounted for only by the notation that "discussion followed on the first Rubric." And the next session "proceeded to further discussion of the Holy Communion Service."[4]

The tenor of these deliberations may be inferred from the situation in which they took place. Given the known interest of many Canadian clergy in restoring the eucharist to something nearer 1549 (usually this meant putting the first of the thanksgiving prayers, the "Prayer of Oblation," after the words

1. *Minutes of the Central Revision Subcommittee, August 28, 1912, and January 8, 1913. Cf. The Book of Common Prayer, Canada, 1918, p. XXIV and p.39. The 1662 rubric ordered "the Litany ... to be sung or said after Morning Prayer upon Sundays..."*
2. *Since the 1850s and 1860s, when the full liturgy at 11 a.m. was still customary (though far from satisfactory, since few stayed beyond the "Ante-Communion" even on the great feasts), High Churchmen had been anxious to separate the eucharist and by so doing increase the number of communicants; Low Churchmen wanted Matins regularized as a separate Sunday service. Cf. Headon, op. cit., p.170.*
3. The Book of Common Prayer, Canada, 1962, p. 707, Articles of Religion XXV, paragraph 1, also p. 550, The Catechism: The Sacraments.
4. *Minutes of the Central Revision Subcommittee, April 4, 1913.*

THE ORDER FOR THE ADMINISTRATION OF

THE LORD'S SUPPER

OR

HOLY COMMUNION

¶ *SO many as intend to be partakers of the holy Communion shall signify their names to the Curate, at least some time the day before.*

And if any of those be an open and notorious evil liver, or have done any wrong to his neighbours by word or deed, so that the Congregation be thereby offended; the Curate, having knowledge thereof, shall call him and advertise him, that in any wise he presume not to come to the Lord's Table, until he have openly declared himself to have truly repented and amended his former naughty life, that the Congregation may thereby be satisfied, which before were offended; and that he have recompensed the parties, to whom he hath done wrong; or at least declare himself to be in full purpose so to do, as soon as he conveniently may.

The same order shall the Curate use with those betwixt whom he perceiveth malice and hatred to reign; not suffering them to be partakers of the Lord's Table, until he know them to be reconciled. And if one of the parties so at variance be content to forgive from the bottom of his heart all that the other hath trespassed against him, and to make amends for that he himself hath offended; and the other party will not be persuaded to a godly unity, but remain still in his frowardness and malice: the Minister in that case ought to admit the penitent person to the holy Communion, and not him that is obstinate. Provided that every Minister so repelling any, as is specified in this, or the next precedent paragraph of this Rubrick, shall be obliged to give an account of the same to the Ordinary within fourteen days after at the farthest. And the Ordinary shall proceed against the offending person according to the Canon.

¶ *The Table at the Communion time having a fair white linen cloth upon it, shall stand in the body of the Church, or in the Chancel, where Morning and Evening Prayer are appointed to be said. And the Priest standing at the north side of the Table shall say the Lord's Prayer with the Collect following, the people kneeling.*

OUR Father who art in heaven, Hallowed be thy Name, Thy kingdom come, Thy will be done, in earth as it is in heaven. Give us this day our daily bread; And forgive us our trespasses, As we forgive them that trespass against us; And lead us not into temptation, But deliver us from evil. Amen.

The beginning of the Communion Service in the 1918 Prayer Book. Note the addition of page numbers.

of institution in the Prayer of Consecration or, alternately, using the Scottish Prayer of Consecration), the debate would likely be about the advisability of touching the eucharist at all for fear of opening up a Pandora's box. Failure to do anything, however, might appear to High Churchmen to be suspiciously close to exhibiting a Low Church bias toward 1552 and, hence, cause trouble. Some judicious change would seem, then, to be in order, except for the additional fact that another group of clergy (both High and Low) had developed a personal rationale of the 1662 rite which suited them, and viewed talk of any change with a jaundiced eye.

As a result, the eucharist went almost untouched. Armitage moved that the whole service from its title to its end be accepted unchanged, and noted later that if he had pressed the matter the motion would have passed and would thus "have saved much heart-burning and misunderstanding."[1]

The Committee, however, resolved to examine the eucharist, and in the discussion following, each part was considered and any action was agreed upon. The outcome was the adoption of a second motion by Armitage, almost identical to the first, but adding 16 items on which agreement for revision had been reached.[2] The changes made at this time were for the most part ratified at the next Committee meeting, and subsequently approved by the General Committee and General Synod. They were all minor, but some were nonetheless liturgically significant.

One of the most significant was the acceptance of the Summary of the Law as a replacement for the Ten Commandments on most Sundays and at "secondary celebrations."[3] Almost immediately its use began to be extended. The *Gloria tibi* and *Laus tibi*, already widely used, were inserted before and after

---

1. Armitage, op. cit., p.245.
2. The basis for the Canadian changes appears to have been The Committee of the Lower House of the Convocation of Canterbury on the Royal Letter of Business of November 10, 1906, The Ornaments, Rubric and Modifications of the Existing Law Relating to the Conduct of Divine Service. Report No. 428 (London, 1909) Resolutions 33, 34, 37, 41 & 46.
3. General Synod, Journal of Proceedings 1915, p.64. cf. The Book of Common Prayer, Canada, 1918, p.268ff.

the Gospel, respectively, thus affording it a ceremonial distinction if so desired. Three Offertory Sentences (less monetary in tone than Cranmer's) were added to the end of the 1662 selection and, from the Scottish Liturgy, a Proper Preface for Epiphany.[1]

Two rubrical alterations bespoke the change in the Canadian church's special status: the rubric governing notices which might be given during the liturgy was altered to recognize the lack of legal status of which the reference to briefs and citations was a remnant,[2] and the ecclesiastical duties rubric left over from the feudal system was replaced with an admonition to "contribute regularly" so that the worship of God might be maintained.[3]

An interesting piece of revision was the addition of a rubric allowing the priest to use both Post-Communion Prayers if he wished. Considering that many clergy wanted the first prayer attached to the Prayer of Consecration, this may have been a gesture in their direction.[4]

The greatest difficulty was caused by the Exhortations.[5] In 1662 the rubric following the Prayer for the Church stated that, on the Sunday or Holy-Day prior to a celebration of the eucharist, "the Minister ... shall ... read this Exhortation" (or the second one if the people were negligent about coming to communion); and during the celebration, when prospective communicants were conveniently placed for receiving the Holy Sacrament, "the Priest shall say this Exhortation" (the third one). In actual fact, the Exhortations were seldom used, and the revisers were undecided about whether to simply rec-

---

1. The Book of Common Prayer, Canada, 1918, pp.269, 273 & 283
2. Ibid. p.270.
3. Ibid. p.291.
4. This prayer was based on the third paragraph of the 1549 Canon and was widely referred to as "the Prayer of Oblation," though in its 1592-1662 form it contained neither an oblation of the gifts nor an epiclesis. Where it was added to the Prayer of Consecration, in defiance of the rubrics, it represented at best a moral victory and kept alive a hope which was eventually fulfilled.
5. Minutes of the Central Revision Subcommittee, April 4, 1913, and September 13, 1913. Minutes of the General Committee, April 28, 1914, General Synod Journal of Proceedings 1915, p.64.

ognize current custom or (in the case of the first Exhortation at least) try to encourage its use again so that people would learn about "the meaning of this Sacrament and its due observance."[1]

Anyone who has worked with the Prayer Book will recognize their dilemma, that of being torn between material of superior quality while having to admit that, for all its inherent worth, it is part of a world gone by. In subsequent meetings over a period of several years, the status of the Exhortations moved between compulsory use, with removal of the penal clauses for blasphemous or hypocritical reception, and compulsory use of the first paragraph of the first Exhortation. In the end, the revisers decided to make all of them optional.[2] They rejected efforts, though, to have them removed to the end of the service.

In a revision that was said to be sane and conservative, the eucharist was handled with the greatest restraint, and charges that little was done are accurate. But that little was not insignificant: the principle of revision was established; the Cranmerian attempt to introduce an orthodox-type of liturgy was abandoned; circumstances were recognized as a just influence on liturgy (as in the provision for local notices); and the hortative elements, so dear to the Reformers and essential to Cranmer's personal sacramental theology, were de-emphasized. Limited, then, by a restrictive mandate and challenged by party tensions, the revisers succeeded in making changes that were either customary already, common sense, or clearly enrichments; and though they only did a little, they did it well.

At the General Synod of 1915, the draft book was presented for approval, and Archbishop Matheson expressed in his charge the "earnest wish" that "this important work ... be carried through at this meeting of our General Synod."[3] This advocacy, apart from the merits of the book itself, was, says Armitage, "probably the chief factor leading to its accep-

---

1. Armitage, op. cit., p.248.
2. Book of Common Prayer, Canada, 1918, pp.275-279.
3. General Synod, Journal of Proceedings 1915, p.15f.

tance."[1] The book was duly adopted by General Synod,[2] but then had to be approved by the Provincial Synods; and here the seriousness of its limited scope became apparent.[3]

Questions were raised about the eucharist (particularly the failure to even consider revision of the Prayer of Consecration), about prayers for the departed,[4] and about the advisability of completing the work before any assessment could be made of the general changes in society being wrought by World War I. The Provincial Synod of Rupert's Land, having no copies of the book to examine and having to rely perforce on Matheson's description of it, accepted the work; but the Provincial Synod of Canada suggested numerous changes and declined, in the end, to accept the 1915 book, other than as a basis for further revision and enrichment.

All comments were forwarded to the Committee, which considered them and incorporated some into a new draft book. On the major items, however, the Committee members could not in good conscience do more than they had already done. With a few alterations, then, the book was once more presented to the General Synod of 1918, and again, Matheson urged its acceptance. The argument, raised by army chaplains and others — that the book had not changed nearly enough to meet the changing society — he denounced as exaggerated, "almost hysterically so."[5] As for the argument that Canada should wait for the motherland, Matheson pointed out that this course of action could have only two possible outcomes: interminable delay while acute divisions of doctrine and prac-

---

1. Armitage, op. cit., p. 85.
2. General Synod, Journal of Proceedings 1915, p.64f.
3. Armitage, op. cit., pp.98-110.
4. Even as the Provincial Synods met in 1916, the dreadful toll of Canadian soldiers was being exacted on the battlefields of France. The pastoral need to comfort grieving families created a desire to pray explicitly for those who had died regardless of possible theological objections.
5. In this Matheson was to be proven wrong. As early as 1910 Lord Esher, advisor to Edward VII, wrote after the dispersal of the great gathering of kings for that monarch's funeral: "There never was such a break-up. All the old buoys which marked the channel of our lives seem to have been swept away." Quoted in Barbara W. Tuchman, The Guns of August (New York, 1962) p.30.

tice were settled, or such drastic change that the church might be irreparably torn apart. The Canadian church, he argued, must settle its own affairs. Again he spoke of his own wish that the work be completed at once, and of the hope of some English bishops that Canada would give a strong lead. Finally he drew attention to another matter at once practical and forceful in its unspoken implications: during seven years of work, the publishers had borne the considerable expenses incurred by the revisers in travel, accommodation, and printing reports and drafts, and the time had come when they should be allowed to recoup this outlay through sales of the revised book.

The new draft passed the General Synod, was approved by the Provincial Synods, and in 1921 returned to General Synod for final ratification. Before the synod even opened, the Upper House, meeting as the House of Bishops, gave its unanimous approval, and when the Lower House assembled, Hague urged them to do the same. But unanimity was not to be. Kerwin Martin, Chancellor of the Diocese of Niagara, objected and insisted that the report of the Committee be read. This done, he began a bitter attack on the work until being shouted down; the report was passed by a large majority.

Martin had followed closely the reports made to the Convocation of Canterbury by the Royal Commission since 1906, and was aware that the Canadian revisers had adopted some of the earlier recommendations but seemed arbitrarily to reject those that came later. This seemingly whimsical policy left many rubrics still honoured more in the breach than observance, and the Prayer Book still full of feudal ideas at a time when great social change seemed imminent. Viewed in this light, Martin's frustration was understandable but impracticable. The kind of revisioning of the church's life and worship which he seems to have had in mind would require another half-century of work before beginning to find expression. The primate was correct. Prayer Book revision, like politics, is the art of the possible; better for the Canadian church to settle for a modest accomplishment now and establish the precedent of revision.

7   *The inter-revision period*

The Prayer Book of 1918 was complete, but there were carry-overs and strong feelings from past dissensions, of which Martin's outburst was only the most evident. In handling the eucharist, the revisers had been careful not to do anything which could be construed as High or Low or anything other than enrichment. But the very refusal to deal with requests such as a change in the Prayer of Consecration made the work appear, to some, to be slanted toward the Low Church view. As a result, for the next two decades, a struggle took place between those who wanted the liturgy as it was (still essentially 1662) and those who wanted it revised in the direction of 1549.

The Focus of Dissent
The heart of the matter, the real issue in Prayer Book revision (both in Canada and in England) was identified by Dyson Hague: "Once more the Church of England is at the parting of the ways.... Once more the centre of the battle is the Communion Service."[1] At the time of the creation of the Prayer Book, Hague said, the storm centre had been the Mass; 1549 got the Church of England half way out of the Mass into the Communion Service, and 1552 took it the rest of the way. The English revision of 1928, one of whose chief features was the restoration of the oblation of the elements in the Canon, was an attempt to restore the old sacramental idea of grace.[2]

---

1. *Dyson Hague*, The Holy Communion Service of the Church of England (*London, undated, but the preface by Bishop Knox would indicate a date prior to 1927*) p.86.
2. *Dyson Hague*, Through the Prayer Book (*London, 1932*) p.391 f. Cf. also Hague, The Protestantism of the Prayer Book, pp. XV-XVI, 41-42 & 53.

This central issue in Anglicanism[1] had been a live issue in Canada for some time and had presented itself when the idea of revision was first broached. In 1911 the Joint Committee received the results of a questionnaire on revision which had been sent to all members of General Synod.[2] Most of the questions were safe enough and elicited little that was controversial, but at the end was a request for "any other suggestions," and responses to this revealed an openness to change (for instance, some requested that the name of the national church be changed to the Anglican Church of Canada). Other suggestions concerned the eucharist and called for changes which would place it at the centre of a strengthened sacramental theology: the separation of the Holy Communion from the Occasional Offices; the addition of Proper Prefaces for a number of Holy Days, along with alternate sets of Collects, Epistles, and Gospels; the reconstruction of the Prayer of Consecration on the lines of 1549; and permission to reserve the sacrament for the sick. The revisers successfully sidestepped these suggestions, but once raised, they were not forgotten nor left dormant.

Two years after the questionnaire, in the summer of 1913, F.W. Vroom of King's College, N.S., delivered to the clergy of the diocese a series of lectures on "Liturgical Principles." Their purpose was to establish some standard by which to judge the draft book which would be making its appearance at the next General Synod. Vroom contrasted the "impatience" of the Canadian revisers to the American church, which had taken twelve years of careful examination to produce its revision of 1892. He particularly commended the suggestion by Bishop Gore of Oxford that time be taken to experiment with legiti-

---

1. Anglicanism, as the definition of a system of Christian belief began to emerge at the time of Elizabeth I as a via media between the opposing factions of Rome and Geneva. It received definition in the 17th century in the lives and writings of Andrewes, Laud, Sparrow, Ken, and others known collectively as the Caroline Divines. Cf. F.C. Cross, ed., The Oxford Dictionary of the Christian Church–Anglicanism (London, 1958).
2. General Committee, Minutes, September 13, 1911.

mate variations and thereby gain practical experience of what was being suggested.[1] In regard to the perceived limitations imposed on the revisers by the guidelines adopted in 1911, particularly as these related to the eucharist, Vroom dismissed the grounds of "no change in doctrine or principles" by pointing out that the same proviso had allowed the American church to adopt the Scottish canon and now allowed the whole bench of English bishops to back proposals of a similar nature.[2] In the published lectures, he scathed the 18-line report of the Canadian revisers as "all that the wit of the Committee could devise in the way of elasticity, enrichment and revision" despite having such examples before them.[3] Personally, Vroom would have liked a complete return to 1549, but his suggestion for the Canadian church was that it follow the recommendations of the report of the Royal Commission which in 1914 received approval of the Lower House of the Convocation of Canterbury: that the "Amen" be omitted at the end of the 1662 Prayer of Consecration, that the first of the post-communion prayers prefaced by "Wherefore" be added to it, and that the Lord's Prayer follow immediately.[4]

Again, after the General Synod of 1915, when the draft book went before the diocesan and provincial synods, similar suggestions were put forward. Memorials from the dioceses of Qu'Appelle, Ottawa, and Quebec urged changes in the Canon, the latter specifically suggesting that action be postponed in order to make use of insights current in other parts of the Anglican Communion.[5] The Provincial Synod of the Ecclesiastical Province of Canada declined to give approval to

---

1. F. W. Vroom, Prayer Book Revision in Canada: Lectures Delivered at the Summer School for Clergy at King's College, Windsor, N.S. (published privately, 1915) p.6-15. These lectures had been repeated in the summer of 1914 by popular request and published subsequent to that.
2. Ibid. p.18
3. Ibid. p.42
4. Ibid. p.44. Cf. also Committee of the Lower House, Convocation of Canterbury on the Royal Letters of Business, Modification of the Existing Law Relating to the Conduct of the Divine Service (London, 1914) p.10.
5. Armitage, op.cit., pp.107-109.

the draft book other than as a basis for further work, and regretted the failure to re-arrange the prayers following the Sanctus according to the Scottish or American form "which follows the model of the Eucharistic Prayer of Consecration in the purest ages of the Church."[1]

But it was all to no avail. The final draft of the Prayer Book passed at General Synod in 1918 with no major work done on the eucharist. A last attempt by Dean Shreve of Quebec at the synod itself was first ruled out of order and postponed, and then simply by-passed on the closing day on the grounds that too few members were left to properly consider such an important matter.

With revision complete and the new book a *fait accompli* but for formal ratification, the majority of church leaders probably thought that eucharistic reform had been given all the attention it was going to get; but they were wrong. If the voices of those favouring eucharistic reform were not listened to, neither were they silenced. Their cause had not in fact been denied by the revisers but, rather, deemed risky at present and without widespread support. What now began was a struggle, on the part of those interested to establish the fact, that a legitimate issue existed and that it merited action.

The Struggle for Further Revision

After 1918, the chief task of the Committee on Prayer Book Revision (as it was now designated) was to promote sales of the new book. And this concern brought to light a quiet campaign of passive resistance amongst those of disappointed hopes. "I presume you are aware that some of our very advanced men have so far completely ignored the existence of the revised book," wrote Archbishop Matheson in 1921, "and have not even made experimental use of it temporarily. I have used the Confirmation Service in the new book ever since it came out but I almost invariably have to take an extra copy with me to

---

1. Report of Action Taken by the Provincial Synod of the Ecclesiastical Province of Canada on the Revised Prayer Book, October 2, 1917. *Resolution No. 15.*

lend to the Anglo-Catholic because he does 'not know the book'."[1]

Such low-keyed resistance might have been both expected and confidently predicted to dwindle in time, but as the 1920s progressed, it persisted and even received new impetus. Thus, in the spring of 1927, Bishop Williams of Huron Diocese feared that sales of the Canadian Prayer Book would suffer if the proposed book of 1928 were to be adopted in England, "because I have no doubt that some of our Anglo-Catholic friends in this country will hold back from buying, in hope of getting a further change in our own Canadian Prayer Book."[2]

Alongside passive resistance and continuing ferment in the Canadian church, there was a growing hope that the "mother church" in England would rescue Canadian Anglicans who were disappointed with the 1918 revision. Archbishop Thornloe, Metropolitan of Ontario and Bishop of Algoma said in his charge to the Provincial Synod of Ontario in 1919: "It is ... a sincere regret to me that the Consecration Prayer ... was not changed to make it more in accord with ... the Scottish and American Churches."[3] These sentiments were echoed a year later by Bishop Lennox Williams of Quebec in his foreword to a book on the subject by Dean Shreve: "I have long felt," wrote Williams, "that our greatest need in the matter of Prayer Book Revision is a re-arrangement of the Holy Communion Office in order that we may have once more restored to us the "Invocation of the Holy Spirit" and the "Prayer of Oblation.""[4]

---

1. The Most Rev. S.P. Matheson, Letter to the Ven. W.J. Armitage on the subject of the Prayer Book. Undated, but internal reference indicates 1921. Now with the Revision Committee correspondence in the National Church Archives, Toronto.
2. The Right Rev. David Williams, Letter to the Ven. W.J. Armitage on the subject of the Prayer Book. Dated March 26, 1927. Now with the Revision Committee correspondence in the National Church Archives, Toronto.
3.The Most Rev. George Thornloe, Charge to the Provincial Synod of Ontario, Session 4, September 16, 1919.
4. The Right Rev. Lennox Williams, in the foreword to the Very Rev. Richmond Shreve, The Prayer of Consecration in the Holy Communion (St. Johns, Quebec, 1920), p.11.

In his book, *The Prayer of Consecration in the Holy Communion*, Shreve began by noting that the principle of allowing options for discretionary use had been established in the 1918 revision, and asked that the American Prayer of Consecration be printed as an option to the present Canadian usage. Such alternate forms, he went on, were already found in the American, Scottish, and Japanese books where they neither caused confusion nor created party spirit.

Shreve then turned to the four objections most often raised against the third paragraph of the Prayer of Consecration. To the argument that the Holy Spirit came only on animate beings and not on inanimate objects (as the epiclesis would have it), Shreve countered by reference to God sending his Spirit upon the waters at creation, the invocation of the Spirit upon the waters of baptism, and the writings of St. Jerome and Theophilus of Alexandria. That the epiclesis could not be traced back past the fourth century was an argument that carried less weight when confronted by elements in the present liturgy which dated only to the sixteenth century (though, in fact, pre-fourth century references could be cited). If the objection that the epiclesis opposed the principles of the Reformation were allowed, Shreve pointed out, whole branches of the Anglican Communion would be condemned. And, finally, in answer to the argument that the concept of oblation was unheard of in the Anglican Communion and would lead to a theology of transubstantiation, Shreve cited a long list of notables who had spoken to the contrary, including Bishop Gore and the report of the Committee of Liturgical Scholars of the English Church Union.[1] In conclusion, he warned, the postponement of change in the Prayer of Consecration was the cause of many clergy acting on their own — a breach of order and discipline, and the start of the introduction of private devotions into the church's common worship.

As always since the 1917 synod of the Province of Canada, Shreve was answering and being answered by an anonymous pamphleteer, well-read in current Prayer Book studies, who

---

1. *Ibid. pp. 12-24.*

believed that efforts to revise the eucharist were part of a secret plot by the clergy to turn the Holy Communion into the Mass.[1] The pamphlets are interesting because for the author the question is not, at heart, a scholarly one, nor do precedents in the Scottish or American churches count for anything. For him the two things that weigh most heavily against revision of the eucharist are that it is non-English and that it conjures up fears of Rome. To many churchmen of the day, these two long-standing fundamentals of Canadian church life were undoubtedly of more significance than appeals to tradition or theology.

From this point of view, Vroom's *An Introduction to the Prayer Book*, written because of "the perplexity in the minds of many of our own people during the unhappy controversy over Prayer Book revision" in England,[2] was a more helpful work than Shreve's. Controversial elements, such as the north-end position of the celebrant, were explained with reference to Prayer Books from 1549 to 1928, along with relevant judicial decisions. Vroom was still pushing for further revision in Canada, but his book spoke more to underlying concerns and helped make what was being asked for a more acceptable thing.

Meanwhile, on another front, revision struggles were continuing, in particular, the procedural struggle to get eucharistic revision before General Synod.

Shreve's motion of 1918 for permission to use the American Prayer of Consecration, having been postponed, came up automatically at the General Synod of 1921. Because of an accident, however, Shreve was absent, thus leaving his motion, once again, as unfinished business.[3] Another motion, however (a request to have the Exhortations removed to a place at the end of the service), was referred to the continuing Joint Committee on Prayer Book Revision, which was to collect all such

---

1. Anonymous, Vital Questions for Canadian Churchmen, *Nos. 1-4. These carry no date or place of publication, but internal references indicate a period between 1917 and 1922.*
2. F.W. Vroom, An Introduction to the Prayer Book *(London, 1930) p.VII.*
3. General Synod, Journal of Proceedings 1921, p.156.

suggestions and make a report on them to General Synod "from time to time."[1] This, of course, would not prevent Shreve's motion from coming before synod again, but it did set a precedent; and in 1924, when Shreve was present and his motion duly appeared for consideration, an amendment was passed that his and all other suggestions on revision be referred as a matter of course to the Standing Committee on Prayer Book Revision. But this time the stipulation was that they "be reported upon *at such time as the Synod may decide upon further general revision of the Prayer Book.*"[2]

This amendment got rid of the issue of revision for the foreseeable future. A majority of General Synod were either satisfied with what they had, or were opposed to the ideas that would be presented if the matter were to be re-opened. And, as a practical consideration, the new books were in print and being bought.

Over the next few years the pro-Revisionists began to realize what a blow had befallen them. At the same time, however, they were spurred on by the Church of England's acceptance of the 1928 Prayer Book with its alternate usages, and by the unpalatable nature of the book's defeat in the House of Commons. A number of English bishops refused to accept this "tyranny" by the state and authorized the book, or parts of it, for use in their dioceses — a move which in the eyes of many Canadian clergy gave 1928 something of the status of a resource from which appealing elements might be drawn. For pro- Revisionists in Canada, such thinking suggested a way round the impasse of the 1924 resolution.

At General Synod in 1931, a memorial from the Diocese of Kootenay requested the synod to authorize for general use in Canada the modified form of the Ten Commandments as set forth in the *Book of Common Prayer*, England 1928,[3] a reasonable request at first glance. The 1918 book presented the Commandments in full, making for a lengthy recitation and result-

---

1. *Ibid. p.*48.
2. *General Synod*, Journal of Proceedings 1924, *p. 32 (my italics)*.
3. *Ibid.* 1931, *p.*443.

ing in them being widely displaced by the Summary of the Law. The 1928 book made the "glosses" in the commandments optional, thereby shortening the recitation by half and, presumably, encouraging greater use of them. To accede to Kootenay's request, however, would have given official recognition to the rejected book (a diplomatic indiscretion, to say the least) and, moreover, would have opened the way to further requests for acceptance of other parts of the book, specifically the Prayer of Consecration.

In the Lower House, vigorous efforts were made to dispose of this memorial by referring it to the Upper House for a decision, or by consigning it to the Committee on Prayer Book Revision. Equally vigorous efforts, however, resulted in the defeat of both proposals. Finally, a motion was made by the secretary of the Committee on Prayer Book Revision, that the request be referred to the House of Bishops for an opinion before the Lower House dealt with the matter.[1] This motion passed, but its intention was then circumvented when the House of Bishops themselves simply referred the matter to the Committee, that "undiscover'd country from whose bourn no traveler returns."

The Diocese of Kootenay raised the issue of the Commandments again at the General Synod of 1934, and the Committee on Prayer Book Revision brought in a report that it was storing up requests, but nothing more could be done.[2] The committee could not bring the matter of revision up for discussion until asked, and clearly a majority of the synod had no intention of doing that.

However, after the synod of 1934, when J.C. Farthing, Bishop of Montreal, became chairman, the Committee itself determined to seek some other means of forcing the synod to respond to the growing pressure for action. When they met in 1935, Kootenay's efforts were furthered by the Diocese of Algoma. Algoma presented a re-written Prayer of Consecration using the 1928 introductory phrase ("All glory be to thee

---

1. *General Synod*, Journal of Proceedings 1931, *pp. 82-84.*
2. *Ibid.* 1934, *p.41.*

...") and preceding the "Prayer of Oblation" with a formal anamnesis and epiclesis, this prayer to be followed by the Our Father with introduction, the Fraction, and the Peace. Vroom's requests were also reiterated. The Committee then decided to draw up a full report on all suggestions received, to be presented at the next General Synod. Their opinion was that the time was ripe to act on these suggestions without undertaking a "general revision" — the category specifically referred to in the 1924 Resolution.[1] A report to this effect was subsequently drawn up[2] but never reached synod, because in the meantime somebody showed the committee "a more excellent way."

At a special meeting in May 1937, the report for General Synod that autumn was "reconsidered."[3] Present were only Bishop Farthing, Principal Waller of Huron College, and Dean Carlisle of Christ Church Cathedral in Montreal who, although a member of the Hymnal Committee, was not a member of the Committee on Prayer Book Revision. Paragraphs one and two of the report, outlining the history of the Committee from its inception in 1921 to its silencing in 1924, remained unchanged in the new report. The bombshell came in the third paragraph, which disclosed the fact that the 1924 Resolution had not been sent to the Upper House for concurrence and was therefore not an act of synod. This being so, the Committee was governed by the original terms of 1921 which ordered it to "report from time to time to the Synod" on its own initiative.[4]

For twenty-two years, from the time the draft book was presented to the General Synod in 1915 with the eucharist unchanged until now, those who wished to keep the 1662 rite had successfully warded off a growing chorus of requests for change. Now, with one brief sentence, their defenses were breached. Not only this, but as events at the 1937 synod would show, the number of defenders had decreased.

---

1. *Committee on Prayer Book Revision, Minutes*, September 16, 1935.
2. *Committee on Prayer Book Revision, Minutes*, September 22, 1936.
3. *Committee on Prayer Book Revision, Minutes*, May 5, 1937.
4. *General Synod*, Journal of Proceedings 1937, p.86.

On the first day, a resolution was passed in the Lower House inviting the Upper House to consider, in joint session, the report of the Committee on Prayer Book Revision. The invitation was sent to the Upper House as "Message S," and a reply stating the time for the meeting was awaited, but no reply came. Next day, the Committee members got a second resolution through the Lower House that consideration of the Report on Prayer Book Revision be made the next item of business of the Joint Sessions. This went to the Upper House as "Message V." The pro-Revisionists could clearly muster a majority in the Lower House, but no reply to either message was among the many others arriving from the Upper House.

Finally, on the seventh day, came a cautious reply agreeing to consider the report in joint session, but with the proviso that the Upper House "reserve to itself the right to record its final decision on this matter in the Upper House."[1] Like wary old bucks sniffing the air for danger to the herd, the bishops were prepared, as in 1905, to unilaterally stop any action which they saw as a threat to the church as a whole.

The initial outcome of the report's discussion was a motion that the Committee prepare a general revision of the Prayer Book containing "such enrichment and adaptation as ... may be necessary to meet the requirements of the Church" and adhering to "the position of the Church of England in Canada laid down in the solemn declaration (sic)."[2] This revision was to be submitted to the next meeting of General Synod.

The motion was made and seconded by delegates from the Province of Canada. The call for a work to be completed in three years might seem odd coming from the same milieu which had so vigorously opposed as hasty the plan to finalize the original revision in 1915. But by now "everyone" knew what was to be done. The Committee would produce a book of the 1928 type with an alternative eucharistic rite, and a few other non-controversial changes which had been suggested over the years. If such a revision passed, it would simply give

---

1. *General Synod*, Journal of Proceedings 1937, *pp.32 and 39*.
2. *Ibid. p.92.*

official status, as an alternate usage, to the sort of things already accepted in some parishes anyway.

In a joint meeting of both the Upper and Lower Houses of synod, however, the pro-Revisionists were still not able to command a majority, so a temporizing amendment was passed which would avoid immediate action and give the Committee a mandate only to "inquire as to the mind of the Church regarding revision of the Prayer Book and make a full report at the next meeting of General Synod."[1] To establish the extent of support among the rank and file of the church was not unreasonable, for while many of the clergy wanted change, they were still a minority. In addition, there was virtually no call for revision among the laity (as there had been prior to 1918), and the bishops were cautious; to appear to give in to High Church pressure would not only revive strife, but would also mark the episcopate as having taken a side in it, if only by default.[2]

In a spirit of "one more river to cross," the Committee met in May of 1938 to write to each diocesan bishop asking for an opinion on the best method of ascertaining the mind of the church in his diocese on the matter of Prayer Book revision. Replies were requested before September when the Committee would hold its regular meeting.[3]

By September, only eight replies of a possible 26 had been received, six from bishops and two from individuals apparently delegated by their bishops to answer for them.[4] Of these, only one bishop suggested a method of ascertaining the mind of the church, another had consulted his diocesan synod, and the others simply expressed their personal opinions concerning revisions. Of the eight replies, six favoured further revision and only two were opposed.

Confronted by this discouraging response, the Committee, at its September meeting, decided to send a second letter ask-

1. *Ibid.* p. 92.
2. *The Most Rev. Howard H. Clark, Interview given to the author on the subject of Prayer Book revision at his home in Toronto on September 19, 1977. (Hereafter called Interview with Archbishop Clark.)*
3. *Committee on Prayer Book Revision, Minutes, May 19, 1938.*
4. *Replies received to the initial request of the Committee, now with the Armitage Papers, Wycliffe College, Toronto.*

ing the bishops for specific suggestions as to how the mind of the church in their dioceses might be discovered, making it clear they were not looking for personal opinion.[1] Pertinent sections, for the sake of clarity, were underlined.[2] This letter, as the replies make clear, was sent, as well, to all Committee members elected at General Synod, most of whom did not attend meetings but presumably had some interest in the matter. This time there were 13 replies, eight from bishops and the rest from Committee members. Only three favoured revision at the present time, two gave no opinion since it was not asked for, and eight opposed doing anything for the time being.[3] The replies make clear that a large part of the church was content with the 1918 revision, and that the fear was still strong that the church could again be torn apart by the party spirit "that was for so long a time, our curse."[4]

There was, however, another side to the matter. Archdeacon Vroom noted that clergy, because of dissatisfaction with the 1918 book, were shortening, omitting, or adding what they pleased to the services. Fr. Palmer of the Society of St. John the Evangelist, in a lengthy reply which was sent to all Committee members, listed 20 examples. Both Vroom and Palmer had similar concerns: "Unless the General Synod uses its right to direct the worship of the Church," Palmer wrote, "every priest will become a law to himself on the ground that Synod refuses to act."[5]

Palmer felt that revision should proceed, but Vroom did not think the time opportune (because of the war imminent in Europe), and suggested that the Canadian bishops authorize other uses, as English bishops authorized the use of 1928. That this course of action was seriously explored is indicated by a notation written later on the bottom of one of the replies re-

---

1. *Committee on Prayer Book Revision, Minutes, Sept. 21, 1938.*
2. *The Rev. G. Abbott-Smith, secretary of the Prayer Book Revision Committee, letter to the Rt. Rev. Philip Carrington on the subject of Prayer Book revision, dated Nov. 29, 1938. Now with the Armitage Papers, Wycliffe College, Toronto.*
3. *Prayer Book Revision Committee, Further Comments, Nos. 9-22.*
4. *Ibid. Nos. 9,12, and 13.*
5. *Ibid. Nos. 12, 14 and 21.*

ceived by the Committee: the House of Bishops would not call into question any bishop who consented to the use of the Prayer of Oblation and the Lord's Prayer after the present Prayer of Consecration, provided parishioners did not object, and as long as the chief service on Sundays and Great Festivals was from the 1918 Book.[1]

In the autumn of 1939 the outbreak of war caused both the meeting of the Committee and the General Synod, scheduled for the following year, to be cancelled. The Committee did meet in September of 1940 and found itself confronted with a difficult task. Its mandate had been, however, to discover the mind of the church regarding Prayer Book revision, and its aim since 1938 had been to gather suggestions from the bishops on how to do this. Only 15 (of 26) bishops had been heard from, and only five had suggested ways of discerning the mind of the church. On the unasked (and unauthorized) question — to revise or not — the combined tally of bishops and Committee members was eight in favour and ten opposed. In addition, less than half those contacted had replied which, on the face of it, appeared as massive indifference. What had also to be considered, however, were the accumulated requests for revision from 1921 on, the unilateral (and often uncritical) revisions by individual clergy, and two new requests for action.

It came down to this: from the potpourri of facts and opinions before it, the Committee itself would have to decide on the mind of the church. The 11 members who met for this task in September 1940 were a group different in character from those who had successfully brought revision back before the church in 1937: five members who favoured revision had either resigned or could not attend, leaving only five pro-Revisionists. Due to the unexpected attendance of some nominal members, the Revisionists were out-voted and a motion was passed that "the mind of the Church is not in favour of revision of the Prayer book at the present time: although the desire

---

1. *Prayer Book Revision Committee, Further Comments, No. 21.*

for eventual revision is widespread."[1] The message, then, to General Synod would be: something at some future date, but nothing now. This time it was the pro-Revisionists who had been out-manoeuvered. There was still, of course, the General Synod to be consulted; before the court of the whole church, the case for revision might still be successfully made. At the General Synod of 1943, the Committee report, written by Bishop Hallam, clearly noted that, as far as it could determine from replies received, "no Bishop and no member of the Committee was in favour of immediate revision," including those who had made suggestions for the future. It concluded by recommending that the work of the Committee continue and that clergy and laity who could give expert help be co-opted as members.[2] This recommendation received unanimous support, and a Joint Committee was established to "take all necessary action, in order to provide for the consideration of the Synod at its next session, of General Proposals, as complete as possible for the revision and enrichment of the *Book of Common Prayer*."[3]

1. *Committee on Prayer Book Revision, Minutes, Sept. 12, 1940. Armitage Papers, Wycliffe College, Toronto.*
2. *General Synod*, Journal of Proceedings 1943, p. 169.
3. *Ibid. p. 21.*

8

The second revision: procedure and people

The General Synod of 1943 not only voted to keep revision alive, they also established a new joint committee: the General Committee on Revision of the Book of Common Prayer, made up of all the Upper House and an equal number (34) from the Lower House.[1] The terms of reference given the Committee, however, were open to interpretation. They could, on the one hand, be interpreted minimally, as a request to provide a list of areas in which revision would be considered desirable at some time. Or, on the other hand, the request for "General Proposals, as complete as possible" could be interpreted as a call for a draft book, the sort of thing envisaged in the original motion in the Committee's report to General Synod of 1937.[2] The view of Bishop Hallam, chairman of the new Committee, is indicated in a letter written just after the synod to Bishop Heathcote of New Westminster: "My understanding regarding the Prayer Book Revision is that the General Revision Committee is to prepare for inclusions (sic) in the next Convening Circular any proposals which they may recommend regarding Prayer Book Revision."[3] In his view the mandate was a general and open-ended one that left a good deal up to him and the Committee. This was a situation which Hallam took care to maintain.

---

1. General Synod, Journal of Proceedings 1943, p.169f.
2. Cf. p. 68 above.
3. The Rt. Rev. W.T. Hallam, Letter to the Rt. Rev. Sir Francis Heathcote on the subject of Prayer Book revision, dated Oct. 21, 1943. Armitage Papers, Wycliffe College, Toronto.

DOUG GRAHAM, THATCHER STUDIO, BRACEBRIDGE

The Right Rev. Philip Carrington, Bishop of Quebec. One of a few bishops responding to a survey by the Committee on Prayer Book Revision, he did not sense much demand for change among Anglicans in Canada, but wrote "there are many points I personally would like to see changed in our present book."

The Rev. Roland Palmer, SSJE. In 1938 Fr. Palmer urged General Synod to take up revision again, or else, he feared, "every priest will become a law to himself on the ground that General Synod refuses to act." For the next twenty-five years he was the heart and soul of Prayer Book revision, a key figure in the work of the Central Revision Subcommittee, and their spokesman to the public. After the book was accepted in 1959, Palmer toured the country promoting it. "This revision," he told clergy in St. Catharines, Ont., "will serve us for the next twenty-five years."

M.T. ROCKY SCHULSTAD, NFLD

(Left) The Rt. Rev. Robert Seaborn. As dean of the Cathedral in Quebec he worked closely with Carrington on things such as the selection of epistles and gospels for the Sundays. If Carrington had the vision, it was often Seaborn who worked out the practicalities which allowed that vision to be implemented.

An Unfolding Mandate

The 1943 terms of reference included no provision for any work beyond its "next session" in 1946, and at the synod of 1946, Hallam did not ask for, nor did the synod suggest, any extension or other authorization for what he was doing. Instead, Hallam presented two completed works (the Baptism of Children and a Penitential Office) and *interim* reports on work being done on the Daily Offices and the Psalter.[1] The implication that there was ongoing work seems to have been accepted by synod without question. The Baptismal Service was authorized for experimental use, and queries or suggestions about it (or any other matter) were to be referred to the secretary of the Committee.[2] In other words, under Hallam, a revision Committee was at work, its proposals were meeting approval, all sides were satisfied, and synod was content to accept his agenda. Thus, at the next meeting in 1949, when some tried to get greater clarification from General Synod of the Revision Committee's mandate, their attempt was quietly by-passed.[3] Not until work on the eucharist was under way at North Hatley in Quebec in 1950, did Hallam request further direction from General Synod. He hoped they would authorize in 1952 the preparation of a draft book for presentation in 1955.[4] The request was approved.

By this time, of course, the Committee had put in years of successful work, had involved people and groups all across the country in specific projects, and had proposals for baptism and marriage services approved by synod and issued for use; at this point, rejection of the request involving revision of the key factor, the eucharist, would have been unthinkable.

---

1. General Synod, Journal of Proceedings 1946, *p.440.*
2. *Ibid. p.69.*
3. *The General Committee on Revision of the Book of Common Prayer, Minute Book B, now in the Archives of the General Synod of the Anglican Church of Canada, Toronto, p. 109. The Minutes of the General Committee and the Central Revision Subcommittee are contained in six volumes designated A, B, C, I, II, III, and will hereafter be referred to as Minute Book A or B or etc.*
4. *Minute Book B, p.169.*

Hallam's Plan of Working

Bishop Hallam kept the Committee free from the plethora of guidelines and restrictions which would surely have resulted from a request to synod for specific direction (what shall we do? how shall we go about it? how much shall be done?), and as the years passed, the wisdom and competence of his leadership won widespread respect. Hallam was able to lead so competently because, after years of work on the Revision Committee, he had a general strategy mapped out, an overall approach which was appropriate for the Canadian church. An indication of his thinking reveals itself in a letter which Hallam received at the outset from Bishop Carrington. Hallam kept the letter, and underlined it here and there.

I feel we should (gradually perhaps) come to certain working principles about Prayer Book Revision. We should be prepared to retrace steps taken in our last revision if that will help us.... We should have our eyes continually on the 1662 Book which is, I take it, the doctrinal standard of our fundamental declarations. We should have a sober conservatism and a courageous modernism where change is ... necessary.

We should also have in mind the feeling of the whole church rather than the propaganda of pressure groups.

1. The demand is for the old Prayer Book made workable....

2. *The purpose of the Prayer Book is to enshrine in noble English the tradition of the universal Church.*[1]

3. The first and greatest task of the Committee will be to get the authoritative and traditional order of prayer and sacrament characteristic of the whole church into such reasonable order as will be most available and acceptable....

4. Our primary object is to deal with the Liturgical Order (as under section 3) to simplify, correct, modernize, rearrange, and perhaps enrich; but without disturbing its doctrinal balance or character....

---

1. *Carrington's italics throughout.*

5. Suggested Lines of Approach. It is possible that a solution of our difficulties might be arrived at by making a clear distinction between the authoritative Liturgical Order ... which was sacrosanct, and ... the place at which the minister might use his discretion, the manner in which it should be done, and to give if required a variety of devotions which could be used....

6. Conclusion. This proposal does not envisage Alternatives....[1]

Some members of the Committee wished to begin work immediately on the eucharist, but about that Hallam also had definite ideas which arose from his reflection on the 1918 Revision. "He thought," said Fr. Palmer, "that in the old revision ... they'd become completely bogged down and so didn't do anything."[2] As a result, he would not allow work on the eucharist until the Committee had found their feet as revisers and got to know each other. As the baptismal service was non-controversial, work began on that. More time was spent on it than necessary, Dr. Armitage believed, and though he felt the results were not especially good, the committee did get practice at revision, and more importantly, developed among themselves a great feeling of rapport.[3] "That was Bishop Hallam's design. We had to learn to trust each other," Archbishop Howard Clark recalled. "That was a conscious choice on his part. He knew what he was doing."[4]

Scope and Principles
The scope of the revision was determined, again without being specified, by the common agreement of the revisers that, in Clark's words, "1918 was an unfinished job." In the case of the

---

1. *The Most Rev. Philip Carrington, Letter to the Rt. Rev. W.T. Hallam, on the subject of revision principles, dated Nov. 13, 1943. Armitage Papers, Wycliffe College, Toronto.*
2. *The Rev. Roland F. Palmer, Interview given to the author on the subject of Prayer Book revision at his home in Toronto on Aug. 22, 1977. (Hereafter referred to as Interview with Fr. Palmer).*
3. *The Rev. Dr. Ramsey Armitage, Interview given to the author on the subject of Prayer Book revision, at his home in Maple, Ont. on Feb. 4, 1978. (Hereafter referred to as Interview with Dr. Armitage).*
4. *Interview with Archbishop Clark.*

ANDREW D. SKILLING, TORONTO

The Most Rev. Philip Carrington and Mrs. Carrington at the Lambeth Conference in 1958. He believed the Prayer Book must be a transcript of the pattern of the apostolic faith and mission as that faith and mission finds expression in a particular time and place.

D. SKILLING, TORONTO

The Rt. Rev. William T. Hallam, chairman of the new revision committee established in 1943. He would not allow work on the eucharist until the Committee had found their feet as revisers and gotten to know each other. Fr. Palmer characterized him as a "foxy grandpa." Until his death in 1956, Hallam guided the work of the Central Revision Subcommittee with an open vision and a firm hand.

"In the hope that those who use it may become more truly what they already are, the People of God...." Archbishop Howard Clark, who wrote these words for the preface of the 1962 book, led the group who produced the 1955 and 1962 versions of the Prayer of Consecration.

1918 book, a resolution of General Synod had prohibited any change in doctrine or principle. That the same resolution now governed the 1959 revisers "was taken for granted but it was never passed."[1] Furthermore, the scope of that resolution was immensely broadened by the Committee's reception of a notice from the House of Bishops of Resolution 78a of the Lambeth Conference of 1948 "that the revisions of the Book shall be in accordance with the doctrine and accepted liturgical worship of the Anglican Communion."[2]

The plan, then, seems to have been to maintain the mandate of 1918, implicitly rather than explicitly, in an attempt to avoid many of the long-held partisan animosities that would, undoubtedly, arise in the wake of any move to re-draft it. This decision created the desired effect of an easier and less-charged atmosphere in which to work.

Structure and Procedure
The first meeting of the General Committee on Revision of the *Book of Common Prayer* was held at St. Hilda's College in Toronto on 16 September 1943. Archbishop Derwyn Owen, as primate, was chairman ex officio. Bishop Hallam, chairman of the former Committee, became vice-chairman of the new General Committee and, by virtue of this, chairman of the forthcoming Central Revision Subcommittee.[3] The new secretary was the Rev. Dr. Ramsey Armitage, principal of Wycliffe College, whose father had been secretary during the first revision.

The General Committee began by reviewing the resolution governing the functioning of the Revision Committee in

---

1. *Ibid.*
2. *Minute Book B, p.85. This not only allowed a broader interpretation of the 1909 Resolution than the 1918 revisers took, it opened the way for the principles of the Solemn Declaration of 1893.*
3. *Hereafter, unless otherwise specified, the designation "Committee" will refer to the Central Revision Subcommittee. If some other group is being referred to it will be specified, e.g., the General Committee, the Rubrics Committee, or a subcommittee, the latter being an offshoot of the Central Revision Subcommittee.*

1918,[1] and as a result adopted a similar arrangement outlined in three resolutions: first, that all subcommittees would work through a Central Revision Subcommittee through which they would report to the General Committee and hence to synod and the public; second, that subcommittees were empowered to secure advice and expert council; and third, that there should be a Central Revision Subcommittee which would report to the General Committee from time to time.[2] In this system the Central Revision Subcommittee was pivotal, and as its membership was crucial to the harmonious and effective work of revision, it required careful handling. A motion was passed for a nominating committee to appoint members to the Central Revision Subcommittee; this nominating committee included the following persons: Archbishop Owen, Bishop Hallam, Principal Armitage, Provost Cosgrave of Trinity College, and Fr. Palmer, S.S.J.E., two of whom would represent Low Church interests, two the High Church, and the primate would act as moderator.[3] Later, Archbishop Clark replaced Cosgrave, but the balance remained even when once, toward the end, Palmer and Armitage alone conferred with the primate on nominating members for the Committee.

In structure then, the committee system was based on that adopted for the 1918 revision, with noteworthy differences. In 1911, when the Central Revision Subcommittee was chosen, a nominating committee of nine reported back their choices to the General Committee, who then added two names from the floor and subsequently elected members.[4] This time, the uncertainties of electing were avoided because the General Committee simply accepted the considered choice of the nominators. In the same spirit, it was agreed that initiatives from diocesan synods, called for in the 1940 report to General Synod and duly recommended, should not be encouraged at this

---

1. Cf. p. 42, above.
2. Minute Book A, p.23.
3. Ibid.
4. Joint Committee on the Enrichment and Adaptation of the Book of Common Prayer, Minutes of the General Committee, Sept. 13, 1911.

stage, but rather, "personal and individual suggestions"[1] should be. By discouraging diocesan initiatives (some of which had been building up for close to two decades), powerful lobbying through these synods was avoided and was replaced by individual or small-group reports, which could be considered for their merit and without political connotations.

Once again, then, the Central Revision Subcommittee was at the helm of revision and, this time, even less dependent on popular influence. Though somewhat oligarchic, the structure was also benevolent. As correspondence between Armitage and Hallam shows, every effort was made to represent different schools of thought and to consider for membership men whose ability showed, or came to show, in the life of the church.[2] It was a structure designed to avoid impulse and demagoguery, and to bring about considered and orderly change.

The first meeting of the Central Revision Subcommittee, which took place on 25 November 1943, quickly established the timing, spirit, and procedure for future meetings. (Sessions of the Committee would usually be arranged at the time of the quarterly meetings of the National Executive.) Members gathered in the board room at Church House in Toronto, around a table piled with the Prayer Books of other branches of the Anglican Church, reference books, reports of subcommittees, and correspondence. Work always began with the Litany, led by Bishop Hallam as the others knelt beside their chairs. Then the minutes of the previous meeting would be read as members checked copies with their own notes, after which correspondence would be heard.[3] On other occasions, when extended conferences took place (such as at North Hatley or Ste. Anne de Bellevue in Quebec) the Committee would begin with Matins, followed by the Holy Eucharist, Mid-day Prayers or the Litany at noon, Evensong at the close of the afternoon, and Compline at night. This gave Committee members an opportunity to try out any proposed alterations, but the main pur-

---

1. *Minute Book A, p.23.*
2. *Dr. Ramsey Armitage, three letters to the Rt. Rev. W.T. Hallam on the subject of membership on the Central Revision Subcommittee, dated 1953-55.*
3. *The Most Rev. Robert Seaborn, Interview given to the author on the subject*

pose (reinforced from time to time by talks from Hallam or Armitage) was to emphasize that they were not engaged in an academic exercise, but rather in clarifying and enriching the manner in which Christ and his body, the church, stand before God.[1]

At that first meeting, Bishop Hallam noted the rules of procedure governing the 1918 Central Revision Subcommittee and suggested for their purposes that:

1. a vote on any change would stand only if all three orders were represented and a quorum present;

2. what was done at one meeting must be confirmed at the following meeting;

3. a motion carried by a two-thirds majority, if reconsidered at the same meeting, could not be negated or amended except by a two-thirds majority.[2]

These rules were followed "in spirit": there never was a number set as a quorum,[3] and on occasion only eight or nine members were present; voting was not always done by orders to insure that all three were represented, and in fact, on three occasions work proceeded with no lay person present. Eventually, the second rule was amended to allow for confirmation at "a following meeting," not necessarily the next one,[4] enabling prolonged consideration of an item or its postponement if an interested member could not attend the next meeting.

At North Hatley, when work on the eucharist finally began, the rules of procedure were "stated by the Chairman" again, but in a revised format which tightened up and improved the procedure. To the first rule was added the requirement that there be a majority of two thirds to make any change in a first

---

(Note 3, page 81, continued) *of Prayer Book revision, at his summer home in Sundridge, Ont. on Aug. 20, 1980. (Hereafter referred to as Interview with Archbishop Seaborn).*

1. *Interview with Fr. Palmer.*
2. *Minute Book A, p.29.*
3. *Interview with Archbishop Clark. (In the first revision a quorum was 12.)*
4. *Minute Book A, p.35.*

draft "but a majority shall suffice for considering a motion." And to the second was added the proviso that "no decisions of the Committee as to alterations in the *Book of Common Prayer* are deemed definitely adopted unless confirmed after consideration at a meeting subsequent to" the circulation of the minutes. Number three remained unchanged.[1] These rules inclined clearly toward the status quo, and the burden of proof lay with those who proposed change, a formulation consistent with the mind of the Committee throughout the work.

An insight into how the Committee conducted its work is provided by a letter from Armitage to Hallam, recommending that work on the eucharist follow the method used for baptism:

1. the chairman would direct all members to consider and study the matter, and be prepared to offer suggestions;

2. the Committee should consider reports by persons or groups previously asked to prepare suggested alternatives;

3. a further report based on the first two steps should be made to the meeting by a subcommittee formed pro tem from the Committee;

4. the Committee would then produce a final draft for the General Synod;

5. if synod approved, this would be allowed for permissive use;

6. a questionnaire concerning it would be sent to all clergy;

7. based on responses to the questionnaires, the Committee would then draw up a final revision;

8. this would go again to General Synod for discussion;

9. again General Synod would authorize its permissive use.[2]

---

1. *Minute Book B, p.165.*
2. *Dr. Ramsey Armitage, Letter to the Rt. Rev. W.T. Hallam on the subject of Committee procedure, dated March 6, 1950. Armitage Papers, Wycliffe College, Toronto. Armitage has overlooked the review function of the General Committee which would precede the report to synod.*

Steps number two and six were key in keeping the Committee in touch with the church, and though difficult to implement, they were conscientiously essayed. The latter in particular (getting feedback on permissive usages) was dependent on the nature and extent of local initiative.

The Committee (though, by its structure, secure from lobbying) did want input. At the first meeting in 1943, it was agreed that members should themselves begin studying the whole range of revision and then, as necessary, seek expert advice or appoint other subcommittees. Because of this process, a great many people contributed input to reports on a wide variety of topics. In addition to these official reports, comments sent to the Committee were read by at least one member, and all important matters were discussed. Armitage, as secretary, was meticulous about correspondence, and the Committee felt they had excellent communication with the church at large and that people knew they had been heard.[1]

The Importance of Rapport in the Committee

Such then were the structure, formal rules of procedure, and agreed upon methods of work. To the General Committee on Revision of the Prayer Book and its numerous levels of subcommittees, these procedures acted as the drive rods of an efficient machine; and the informal attitudes and assumptions of the key movers served as the lubricant, enabling a smooth operation rather than a laboured "grinding it out." In the Central Revision Subcommittee, Hallam quickly and consistently established his authority. On receipt of the very first set of minutes, he noted the omission of some suggestions he had made and wrote the secretary tartly to inquire if this had been done

---

1. *Interview with Archbishop Clark. The church at large did not always share this sentiment. The restriction on diocesan input put too great an onus on poorly organized local initiative.*

on the advice of the primate.[1] More than ten years later, he was still holding the reins firmly, wondering what Palmer and Armitage were up to in an unscheduled meeting with Anglican Action, a Toronto-based High Church pressure group.[2] The relationship between chairman and secretary was important, and had always been close and co-operative in the previous revision committees. Fortunately, the relationship between Hallam and Armitage continued in this pattern, as attested to in letters from Armitage to Hallam.[3]

This open and supportive relationship extended into the Committee at large. "One of the miracles under Hallam" Archbishop Clark recalled, "was that we became a homogeneous group."[4] "The most important thing about the Revision work," Palmer wrote in a Queen's College occasional paper, "is the spirit in which it is done.... When anyone proposed a change he was always quite frank about the implications of that change. There has been trust and a mutual effort at understanding all along. We sometimes divided on matters of principle."[5] "Our great object always," he said later, "was to come to a common mind. We never did anything of importance if there was going to be a minority that were very much against a thing."[6]

One of the great dangers, of course, was the easy, but tempting and deadly, road of prefabricated party-thinking. At the first meeting of the Committee, as members came into the board room at Church House, Armitage called Palmer to an empty seat beside him, "where I can keep an eye on you," he said.[7] The two sat side by side after that, but the important

---

1. *The Rt. Rev. W.T. Hallam, Letter to Dr. Ramsey Armitage, dated Oct. 21, 1943. Armitage Papers, Wycliffe College, Toronto.*

2. *Dr. Ramsey Armitage, Letter to the Rt. Rev. W.T. Hallam, dated July 29, 1954. Armitage Papers, Wycliffe College, Toronto.*

3. *Dr. Ramsey Armitage, Letters to the Rt. Rev. W.T. Hallam, written between 1952 and 1955. Armitage Papers, Wycliffe College, Toronto.*

4. *Interview with Archbishop Clark.*

5. *The Rev. R.F. Palmer, "Prayer Book Revision," Queen's College Occasional Paper, No.2, May 1955.*

6. *Interview with Fr. Palmer.*

7. *Interview with Dr. Armitage.*

thing was that they determined there and then that partisan concerns must not be allowed to intrude upon the work of revision. Each had an influence over various people in the church, Palmer said, but both worked hard to put down "stupid party rivalry."[1] Within the Committee, at least, this endeavour achieved success by the time the critical work on the eucharist was reached. "The thing was," said Archbishop Clark, "we had come to the point where we weren't worrying about these little shibboleths of the Reformation, and little shibboleths of the Anglo-Catholics didn't matter to us at all."[2]

In between sessions, Armitage and Palmer habitually "talked things over," reviewing what had gone on and discussing items that lay ahead on the agenda. "We agreed with one another," Palmer remarked, "that we would always talk over any controversial thing before it came up in the committee, and we would find out what would be possible."[3] As a result, they would sometimes come to an agreement beforehand that would avoid a lot of debate for the committee. Monk and minister would be of one mind, and therefore no posturing was needed for the sake of appearances. In the matter of prayers for the departed, for example, Armitage agreed that some good ones proposed for optional use would be preferable to the sentimental or "blood and thunder" ones from medieval sources being presently used by some clergy.[4] This thinking held in the introduction of the term "Holy Eucharist."

A lot, in fact, was done outside the formal sessions. Individuals given a specific job would talk it over with others, and often a solution would be arrived at from the interchange. On one occasion, Clark was asked to produce a better response for the versicle, "Give peace in our time, O Lord." He spent hours searching high and low, tried inventing alternatives, and got nowhere. Then in casual conversation with Palmer, he asked

---

1. *Interview with Fr. Palmer.*
2. *Interview with Archbishop Clark*
3. *Interview with Fr. Palmer.*
4. *Ibid.*

what a good response might be to "Give peace in our time, O Lord." "And evermore mightily defend us," Palmer replied.[1]

The committee then, was set in a firm structure and governed by fairly tight rules. But as the members worked together over time, the formal selection procedures were enhanced by the informal rapport that developed within the committee. An inner group emerged fairly quickly made up of men whose special abilities, interests, and opportunities made them leaders; there were "about a dozen of us," Fr. Palmer recalled, of whom some specialized almost entirely on particular projects for which their education or experience suited them.[2]

Among the inner group there was a recognized core of leaders whose work and decision-making were mainly responsible for getting the job done. These were Bishop William T. Hallam, Archbishop Philip Carrington, Dr. Ramsey Armitage, and Fr. Roland Palmer.

Within the committee, then, a freedom developed which, relying on the security of the structure, allowed people to lower facades and deal face to face with what truly concerned them all — the hope, as Archbishop Clark put it so well, that those who used the revised book might "become more truly what they already are: the People of God, that new Creation in Christ which finds its joy in adoration of the Creator and Redeemer of all."[3]

---

1. *Interview with Archbishop Clark.*
2. *Interview with Fr. Palmer.*
3. The Book of Common Prayer, *Canada, 1959, p. VII.*

¶ *Then shall this general Confession be made, in the name of all those that are minded to receive the holy Communion, by one of the Ministers; both he and all the people kneeling humbly upon their knees and saying:*

ALMIGHTY God, Father of our Lord Jesus Christ, Maker of all things, Judge of all men : We acknowledge and confess our manifold sins and wickedness, Which we from time to time most grievously have committed, By thought, word, and deed, Against thy Divine Majesty. We do earnestly repent, And are heartily sorry for these our misdoings. Have mercy upon us, most merciful Father; For thy Son our Lord Jesus Christ's sake, Forgive us all that is past; And grant that we may ever hereafter Serve and please thee In newness of life, To the honour and glory of thy Name; Through Jesus Christ our Lord. Amen.

¶ *Then shall the Priest (or the Bishop, being present) stand up, and turning himself to the people, pronounce this Absolution.*

ALMIGHTY God, our heavenly Father, who of his great mercy hath promised forgiveness of sins to all them that with hearty repentance and true faith turn unto him: Have mercy upon you; pardon and deliver you from all your sins; confirm and strengthen you in all goodness; and bring you to everlasting life; through Jesus Christ our Lord. Amen.

¶ *Then shall the Priest say:*

Hear what comfortable words our Saviour Christ saith unto all that truly turn to him:

COME unto me all that travail and are heavy laden, and I will refresh you.
St. Matthew 11 : 28

So God loved the world, that he gave his only-begotten Son, to the end that all that believe in him should not perish, but have everlasting life.
St. John 3 : 16

Hear also what Saint Paul saith:

This is a true saying, and worthy of all men to be received, that Christ Jesus came into the world to save sinners.
1 Timothy 1 : 15

Hear also what Saint John saith:

If any man sin, we have an Advocate with the Father, Jesus Christ the righteous; and he is the propitiation for our sins.
1 St. John 2 : 1, 2

¶ *After which the Priest shall proceed with THE THANKSGIVING.*

THE PEACE of the Lord be with you.

Answer: And with thy spirit.

Priest: Lift up your hearts.

Answer: We lift them up unto the Lord.

Priest: Let us give thanks unto our Lord God.

Answer: It is meet and right so to do.

¶ *Then shall the Priest turn to the Lord's Table, and say:*

IT is very meet, right, and our bounden duty, that we should at all times, and in all places, give thanks unto thee, O Lord, Holy Father, Almighty, Ever-lasting God.

¶ *Here shall follow the proper Preface, according to the time, if there be any specially appointed; or else immediately shall follow:*

THEREFORE with Angels and Archangels, and with all the company of heaven, we laud and magnify thy glorious Name; evermore praising thee, and saying:

Holy, holy, holy, Lord God of hosts, heaven and earth are full of thy glory : Glory be to thee, O Lord most High.

PROPER PREFACES

¶ *Upon Christmas Day, and until New Year's Day, and upon the Festivals of the Purification and the Annunciation.*

The 1952 eucharistic rite was issued as a report to be read, but was not allowed to be used.

9   *The 1952 rite*

The revisers who began work on the eucharist were well prepared. They recognized that the more than seven years they had taken to revise other parts of the Prayer Book were the prelude to their chief *"raison d'etre"*:[1] the revision of the eucharist.

Development of the Rite

Immediate preparation for revising the eucharistic rite had begun in the fall of 1949 when Bishop Hallam and Fr. Palmer were asked to do a "preliminary study." The result of this study was a "Questionnaire," in reality a lengthy memorandum, outlining items and issues that needed consideration. Every member of the Central Revision Subcommittee received a copy of this in time to allow for four months of study.[2] Then, in early June of 1950, work on the eucharist was begun. For this important first step, the Committee secluded itself for almost a week at Quebec Lodge in North Hatley, Quebec.

The major resources used by the revisers at this meeting were the 1918 Prayer Book and the Hallam-Palmer questionnaire. The questionnaire noted the elements of the liturgy to be considered, the questions raised about each of these, and provided a number of alternatives, some of which were identified as coming from other Prayer Books — American, South African, or English 1928.

In most cases, the task of the Committee was to decide whether or not any change should be made, which of the alter-

---

1. *General Synod,* Journal of Proceedings 1952, p.294.
2. *Minute Book B, pp.127-161. (Hereafter this memorandum is referred to as the questionnaire).*

natives to select if there were to be a change, and finally, to "fine tune" the wording of the alternative chosen so that it would be said well and in a way that was suitable to the Canadian church. Sometimes in discussion, other points were raised and acted upon, such as the "eleventh commandment"[1] — "Hear also what our Lord Jesus Christ saith: A new commandment I give unto you, love one another." But for the most part, the 1952 rite was determined by the questionnaire.[2]

Careful in preparing for their work, the revisers were equally careful in its execution. The liturgy drawn up at North Hatley was revised by the Committee in the fall of 1951 and again in the winter of 1952. Finally, in May of 1952, the work was scrutinized once more at a meeting of the General Committee. Only then was the resultant rite considered ready for presentation to the General Synod which was to meet in September of that year.[3]

The outcome — the rite of 1952 — embodied 19 significant changes, and set the Canadian liturgy apart as distinct from that of other branches of the Anglican Church.

A Sense of Accomplishment

The revisers felt they had done well. During the summer of 1952, Palmer and Hallam exchanged letters in which they expressed their satisfaction with the 1952 rite.[4] They were particularly pleased with the Prayer of Consecration, to which they had added a third paragraph. The paragraph was not adapted from the Scottish-American model or achieved by adding the "Prayer of Oblation" (i.e., the first of the post-com-

---

1. Cf. p. 104 below.
2. For a detailed discussion of the work see W.R. Blott, "The Influence of the Most Reverend Philip Carrington, Archbishop of Quebec, in Revising the Liturgy of the Book of Common Prayer 1959 Canada," an unpublished M.A. thesis.
3. Minute Book B, p.161f.
4. The Rev. R.F. Palmer, S.S.J.E. Letters to the Right Rev. W.T. Hallam, on the subject of Prayer Book revision, dated June 19 and August 14, 1951, now with the Armitage Papers, Wycliffe College, Toronto, Ont. The Right Rev. W.T. Hallam. Draft of a letter to the Rev. R.F. Palmer, S.S.J.E., on the subject of Prayer Book revision, undated, now with the Armitage Papers, Wycliffe College, Toronto, Ont.

munion prayers in the 1662 book), but was one of their own devising. Hallam especially liked the *anamnesis*[1] and the overall Trinitarian balance. Palmer said in a letter to the *Canadian Churchman* (the national newspaper of the Anglican Church of Canada) that it contained references to all the matter found in the longer forms of the prayer with the exception, he admitted, of the *epiclesis*. He believed, however, that for Canadian Anglicans the words of institution would always be the climax.[2] Palmer considered that the Roman canons, the Orthodox anaphoras, and the 1549 eucharistic prayer did gather all the ideas about the eucharist into one prayer, but at the cost of becoming complicated. The 1952 model, he wrote to Hallam, suggested all the ideas in a word or two and left the thought to be expanded in some other part of the service.

In their report to General Synod, the Committee recommended that copies of the 1952 rite be printed and distributed for comment and suggestion from the church at large. They further reported the work of revision to be sufficiently far advanced that production of a draft book for the next General Synod in 1955 would be possible.[3]

The Committee's report to the synod expressed a sense of achievement and satisfaction. They had worked long, hard, and conscientiously, and had mercifully avoided the threat of party strife (feared so greatly when work began in 1943). In addition to their refusal of the easy path of adopting one or other of the ready-made solutions proposed by different groups, they had risen above partisan factions to strive together for the good of the church as a whole. The long apprenticeship had produced a good and distinctive revision, and the resulting rite was finally released in 1952 "for information and study."[4] There was no inkling then of the avalanche of criticism to come.

---

1. For an illustration of the meaning of these technical terms see page 92, below.
2. The Rev. Roland F. Palmer, S.S.J.E., Letter to the Rev. M.C.D. Hutt, The Canadian Churchman, Vol. 80, No. 1 (January 1, 1953) p.2.
3. General Synod, Journal of Proceedings 1952, p.294.
4. Ibid.

¶ *When the Priest, standing at the Lord's Table, hath so ordered the Bread and Wine, that he may with the more readiness and decency break the Bread before the people, and take the Cup into his hands; he shall say THE PRAYER OF CONSECRATION, as followeth:*

BLESSING and glory and thanksgiving be unto thee Almighty God, our heavenly Father, who of thy tender mercy didst give thine only Son Jesus Christ to take our nature upon him and to suffer death upon the Cross for our redemption; who made there (by his one oblation of himself once offered) a full, perfect, and sufficient sacrifice, oblation and satisfaction, for the sins of the whole world; and did institute, and in his holy Gospel, command us to continue, a perpetual memory of that his precious death, until his coming again.

Hear us, O merciful Father, we most humbly beseech thee; and grant that we receiving these thy creatures of bread and wine, according to thy Son our Saviour Jesus Christ's holy institution, in remembrance of his death and passion may be partakers of his most blessed Body and Blood; who, in the same night that he was betrayed, ᵃtook Bread; and, when he had given thanks, ᵇhe brake it, and gave it to his disciples, saying Take, eat; ᶜ this is my Body which is given for you : Do this in remembrance of me. Likewise after supper he ᵈtook the Cup: and, when he had given thanks, he gave it to them, saying, Drink ye all of this; for ᵉthis is my Blood of the new Covenant, which is shed for you and for many for the remission of sins : Do this, as oft as ye shall drink it, in remembrance of me.

a Here the Priest is to take the Paten into his hands:

b And here to break the Bread:

c And here to lay his hand upon all the Bread:

d Here he is to take the Cup into his hands:

e And here to lay his hand upon every vessel (be it Chalice or Flagon) in which there is any Wine to be consecrated.

Wherefore, O Lord and heavenly Father, in union with all thy holy Church, we do this in remembrance of him who died, and rose again, and ever liveth to make intercession for us, presenting unto thy divine Majesty this our thank-offering and service, through the merits and mediation of thy beloved Son, Jesus Christ our Lord, by whom, and with whom, in the unity of the Holy Spirit, all honour and glory be unto thee, O Father Almighty, world without end. *Amen.*

¶ *Then shall the Priest kneel down at the Lord's Table, and after a short period of silence shall, together with all that shall receive the Communion, humbly say this prayer following:*

WE do not presume to come to this thy Table, O merciful Lord, Trusting in our own righteousness, But in thy manifold and great mercies. We are not worthy so much as to gather up the crumbs under thy Table. But thou art the same Lord, Whose property is always to have mercy : Grant us therefore, gracious Lord, So to eat the flesh of thy dear Son Jesus Christ, And to drink his blood, That our sinful bodies may be made clean by his body, And our souls washed through his most precious blood, And that we may evermore dwell in him, And he in us. Amen.

¶ *Then shall the Minister first receive the Communion in both kinds himself, and then proceed to deliver the same to the Bishops, Priests, and Deacons, in like manner, (if any be present,) and after that to the people also in order, into their hands, all meekly kneeling. And, as he delivereth the Bread, he shall say:*

THE Body of our Lord Jesus Christ, which was given for thee, preserve thy body and soul unto everlasting life : Take and eat this in remembrance that Christ died for thee, and feed on him in thy heart by faith with thanksgiving.

¶ *And the Minister that delivereth the Cup shall likewise say:*

THE Blood of our Lord Jesus Christ, which was shed for thee, preserve

The 1952 Prayer of Consecration. *Unlike the 1549 Eucharistic Prayer (or its equivalents in the Roman Catholic mass and Othodox liturgies), it did not attempt to be a summation of eucharistic theology, but rather, said Father Palmer, suggested the ideas in a word or two and left the thought to be expanded in some other part of the service. So here, for example, the* anamnesis *is simply, "We do this in remembrance of him who died, and rose again, and ever liveth to make intercession for us..."; and the* oblation, *"presenting unto thy divine majesty this our thank-offering and service..." There is no* epiclesis, *i.e., an invocation either of God that he will send the Holy Spirit, or of the Spirit directly, to consecrate the oblation.*

10   *Reaction to the 1952 rite*

On 6 February 1953, six months after the General Synod had approved the 1952 rite for study by the church at large, the members of the Central Revision Subcommittee gathered for a meeting. Their mandate now was to present a draft Prayer Book to the next synod in 1955, for which Bishop Hallam had prepared a strategy. Fourteen other subcommittees had been appointed, each with a particular part of the Prayer Book to work on. The Central Revision Subcommittee would receive their reports for study, and occupy itself further with matters ancillary to the eucharist. As for the liturgy itself, it would not be touched until the February meeting of 1954, in order to give the church time to examine it and communicate its reaction.

In the minutes of the meeting of February 1953, it is noted that comments and criticisms had been received from across Canada, including those voiced in letters to the editor in *The Canadian Churchman*. The responses fell generally into three categories.[1]

The first group had begun to come in quickly, and focused on specific items in the 1952 rite. The Prayer of Consecration was the primary focus of these comments. It had no *epiclesis*, no oblation, and an "indescribable" *anamnesis*;[2] Although its theology could be interpreted as orthodox, the general reader might not interpret it as such. The very language was flat and insipid, indicating nothing of the transcendent mystery of the sacrament. Many suggested that, instead of adopting the 1952 prayer, it would be better to add the "Prayer of Oblation" to the

---

1. Cf. Blott, *op. cit.*, pp. 46-59.
2. Cf. *Illustration p.92 for these terms.*

1662 prayer, or for that matter, to simply stick with the 1662 prayer alone.

A second set of responses criticized the rite as a whole. It showed no understanding of eucharistic theology or the action of the eucharist,[1] and by virtually ignoring revisions in other parts of the Anglican Communion, it set the Canadian church apart. Some in this group favoured *The Proposed Canadian Eucharist*, published about the same time as the 1952 rite, by Fr. Hawkes, S.S.J.E., in the society's paper. This rite (following the lines Vroom had proposed in 1915) made use of traditional material already in extensive use among Anglican churches. Others primarily vented their feelings of frustration and suspicion — after years of work to get the eucharist revised, their concerns were being fobbed off with a few questionable enrichments. These High Church critics perceived, here, questionable machinations of the Low Church. Once again old party animosities showed their continuing strength, and the spectre arose of a revised rite lying ignored while the Low Church factions stuck (more or less) to 1918 and the High Church added the "Prayer of Oblation" or "enrichments" from other sources.

The third and most trenchant set of criticisms of 1952 pointed out that the revisers demonstrated little awareness of both the unsatisfactory theology behind the 1552-1662 rite and the changes which had occurred in society since those distant agrarian times. The method by which they worked — seeking to enshrine the thinking of a few rather than making use of elements which had won popular support over the years — was at fault.

All in all, the message was clear enough. The 1952 rite was too little for those who had wanted a revision, unappealing to those who were satisfied with some form of the 1918 Prayer Book, and liturgically unsuitable to all who had any special knowledge in the field. The Committee found itself back at square one, so to speak. As the secretary, the Rev. Dr. Ramsey Armitage, put it in an article in the *Pan Anglican*: "In the work

---

1. Gregory Dix, *The Shape of the Liturgy*, *had been in print for over six years and was a major factor in appraising new rites*.

of producing a new Canadian Prayer Book it is to the eucharist that the most intensive study must yet be given."[1]

---

1. *The Rev. Dr. Ramsey Armitage, "Canadian Prayer Book Revision,"* Pan Anglican, *Vol. IV, No. 2 (October 1953) p.20.*

Central Revision Sub-Committee
on Revision of the Book of Common Prayer.

/11 Members of the Committee are requested
to study this Memorandum which has been
submitted by the Archbishop of Quebec

ON THE REVISION OF THE EUCHARISTIC LITURGY

The draft of a revised service of Holy Communion put out in 1952 has been very successful in creating a public interest, and in eliciting criticisms and suggestions. We ought to be well-satisfied with this response. The major contributions should be tabulated, showing the reaction of each to the more important points.

In considering the points which have been raised, I cannot help wondering whether our Committee is now sufficiently representative of all points of view. I would welcome at least one representative of the modern Anglo-Catholic point of view, even though I do not always feel sympathetic with it myself. Nor do I quite know where we would look for advice on liturgical points. We have all read some liturgiology, but are we abreast of modern study? Unfortunately, as I consider in my mind some men I know of who have interested themselves in the subject, I cannot help thinking that they seem to be rather too devoted to the propagation of particular theories or points of view. I would not care to have our committee invaded by such propagandists, though their value to us, outside the committee, is undoubtedly very great.

General Policy Our mandate from the Canadian Church has never suggested that there
is a general demand for drastic changes. Our own interpretation of it has been to revise the Prayer Book in such a way as not to disturb the devotional · life of the congregation which uses it; to leave it in all essentials very much the same; and above all not to take away phrases or features which have become familiar.

I do not think that any familiar phrase or feature should be deleted, transformed, or transposed, unless an exceedingly strong case can be made out for doing so

I do not think we should take into account at all the pressure which is brought to bear by active groups with special points of view, unless we are convinced that the changes they ask for are right and wise in themselves, and would be welcomed in the church at large.

The fact that a certain change has already been introduced should leave us cold. As I was told at a gathering of clergy, we are not revising the Prayer Book for the benefit of that class of church, but for the great majority.

Introit Prayers The opening Our Father is an example of a familiar devotion which
should not be taken away. It is the one occasion on which the congregation hears the Our Father, that is if the priest says it audibly as he is told to do; on all other occasions it is repeated by the whole congregation, sometimes rather perfunctorily. The two repetitions in our service, in two different ways, is a stroke of liturgical genius. And it enables the priest to begin the service on the highest possible level.

The Commandments I was impressed by the emphasis on the Old Testament in some of the
briefs which I read. The stupid hostility to the Old Testament seems to be going. Actually Christian liturgy is simply Hebrew liturgy with the gospel. There are no other sources. And the Ten Commandments, like the Shema, are Hebrew liturgical texts which passed directly into the apostolic church as fundamental formulas, with the sanction of our Lord.

The Carrington memorandum renewed the revisor's sense of direction after the church rejected the proposed 1952 rite. Many changes introduced in 1952 remained, such as the softening of the Confession by the omission of the phrase: "The remembrance of them [our sins] is grievous unto us; The burden of them is intoler-able." Other innovations, such as having the exchange of the Peace begin the dialogue before the Preface and Sanctus, were dropped.

11   *The Carrington proposal*

These criticisms placed the Committee in a difficult position. The door of eucharistic revision, once more opened, could not again be shut — there was no going back to the rite of the old Prayer Book. Nor did Anglicans in Canada want an idiosyncratic "Canadian" liturgy. If this much was clear, however, it was less evident what people did want, and how much change would be acceptable. It might have seemed that, since the Committee had asked for comment and received it, they should proceed to analyze it and act on it. But this they dared not do. Within the Committee, a remarkable degree of harmony had been achieved among members of various schools and parties even if, in the church at large, old rivalries and suspicions lived on (dormant to a large degree, but strong and capable of erupting). To have produced a revision perceived as influenced by any one group of critics would have destroyed the Committee's credibility as a body representative of the whole church, and would have doomed its work to failure. In fact, such a course of action might have jeopardized the possibility of revision for years to come.

The Committee's initial reaction to the criticism, then, was to remain studiously aloof and allow it to run its course. In the face of incipient rejection, however, this policy of detachment wavered and then broke. The secretary's statement in the October issue of the prestigious journal *Pan Anglican* (see above) was the first official recognition that the 1952 rite was unsatisfactory. But a one-line reference was hardly enough to deal with the level of reaction taking place in the Canadian church, and two months later, it was felt necessary to call a special meeting of the Committee (28 to 31 December 1953).

At this meeting, the first item of business recorded in the minutes is the reading by the chairman of a statement for public release. It declared that no Prayer Book would be possible for a few years. Apart from the time needed by the Committee for revision of the 1952 rite, the canons of the church required that a draft copy be submitted for examination, amendment, and approval at one meeting of the General Synod. If accepted, it must then be ratified by a following meeting three years later, and finally, it would have to be passed to the Provincial Synods for their approval. The public statement was an assurance that the Committee recognized the dissatisfaction with the 1952 rite, and that due process would allow six to eight years for consideration of any new proposal.

Apart from the fact that it had to be issued at all, the Committee's statement was calm and reassuring, but the circumstances of the meeting indicate the urgency that was felt as the deadline for the draft book drew near: the meeting itself was unscheduled; the time (between Christmas and New Year's Day) was awkward; only nine members could attend; and although no laity were present, the rules of procedure were by-passed and some changes were made.[1]

It seems fortuitous in hindsight that, in the midst of these unusual goings-on, a "communication" was received from Bishop Carrington, who had been unable to attend. It was, the minutes note, "of such weight and importance" that further changes in the rite were postponed. This communication was a memorandum in which Carrington outlined his thoughts on the nature and scope of eucharistic revision. After some consideration, the Committee decided to send a copy to all its members and to postpone any further meeting until the spring.

The Carrington memorandum was not at once appreciated for the seminal document that it was. The initial response of the Committee seems to have been to regard it as a sort of blue-print for revision or a presentation of particulars for their consideration. A case in point is the handling of the Prayer of Consecration in which, at first, a specific proposal of

---

1. Blott, op. cit., p.63f.

Carrington's was adopted almost in its entirety. Later, the wording was greatly changed, but the concept was retained, and this signaled a significant development in approach to the document itself. As the Committee worked with it, and began to appreciate its underlying ideology, they came to realize that the memorandum was less a source of specific suggestions than a model for their project, a document whose premises were based on an understanding of the Anglican Communion, and an appreciation of its situation in the post-World War II era.

Carrington's perceptiveness was based generally on his wide-ranging knowledge of the historic development of the Anglican Communion and, specifically, on his work at the Lambeth Conference of 1948 and the Anglican Congress of 1954.[1] At Lambeth, the two major issues seen to be confronting the church in the post-war world were nationalism and ecumenism, both of which would have to be approached positively, if cautiously, in a manner which would not fragment Anglicans and attenuate their contribution to development of post-war society. In the report on the Anglican Communion, written by Carrington, it was recognized that, among the multifarious groups of churches making up the Communion, unity of faith and order, of purpose and spirit, was found in and expressed by the 1662 Prayer Book. Particularly, it was noted, liturgy is the crucible in which various digressive elements are fused and unified in the fellowship and power of the Holy Spirit.

At the Anglican Congress of 1954 the theme was "The Call of God and the Mission of the Anglican Communion." Carrington, speaking on the structure of Anglicanism, elaborated on the Lambeth statement. The Prayer Book, he said, was the outward expression of the Christian life and, thus, in the absence of any juridical or political structure, the principal institutional factor governing and maintaining the unity of Anglicans. Prayer Book revision, then, could not be approached by any branch of the church as an isolated or one-di-

1. *Blott, op. cit., pp.65-91. The memorandum appeared prior to the Congress but was based on views he and others were to express there.*

mensional activity. Rather, it must meet two criteria: it must be a transcript of the pattern of the apostolic faith and mission as it had found valid expression in a particular time and place; and it must maintain the unity of the Body of Christ by creating mutual recognition which would lead to admission to Communion — in other words, it could not be insular. Massey H. Shepherd of the Church Divinity School of the Pacific, and D. Colin Dunlop, Dean of Lincoln Cathedral, endorsed Carrington's viewpoint, thus reinforcing its impact on the Canadian revisers, especially in areas specific to eucharistic revision and trends in world-wide revision. It became clear that future changes should be modest in scope, should keep as much of the familiar as possible, and should aim at establishing a single authorized rite within which alternatives would be allowed.

The effect of all this on the Canadian revisers may be seen in a remark Bishop Hallam made to Fr. Palmer about the language of the Prayer of Consecration, on his return from the Congress where he seems to have been completely won over: "But the words 'precious death, mighty resurrection and glorious ascension' are more emphatic than 'he died and rose again.' There is a worthiness and nobility about them. I note that they are in practically all the revisions."[1]

Hallam was not the only one impressed. Following the special Christmas meeting at which the Committee had first received Carrington's memorandum, the next consideration of the eucharist was at a meeting shortly before the Congress. This had been a tense and contradictory session, prompting a letter by one member warning of a reactionary and divisive spirit coming into the Committee. By contrast, the meeting of the General Committee two months after the Congress was noteworthy for its common mind and for the uncharacteristically large and significant number of changes introduced and approved. A long road lay ahead still, but now there was confi-

---

1. *The Right Rev. William T. Hallam, Draft of a letter to the Rev. Roland F. Palmer on the subject of the Prayer of Consecration, dated "after September/ before Toronto meeting 1954," now with the Armitage Papers in Wycliffe College, Toronto, Ont.*

dence that they were on the right track and could get on with their work.

The memorandum, then, was not a list of suggestions opportunistically conceived to win approval where 1952 had failed. It was a guide-post pointing the way, a plan of approach to the problem of revision, based on soundly thought-out and widely-held ideas about the place and role of the *Book of Common Prayer* in Anglicanism. It was a statement of principles designed to keep the Canadian church within the framework of ongoing revision in the world-wide church while, at the same time, contributing to the process and avoiding what its revision threatened to become at the end of 1953 — a provincial reaction to local pressures.

The fruits of this work appeared in the draft book of 1955 and received general approval. Some specific changes, however, were recommended, and in its final form the rite was what was presented to General Synod in 1959.

12

Analysis of the 1962 revision

Title Page (p. 65)

T The concept of a title page came from the comments on the 1952 rite, the only debate being over the terms to be used. The proposal to follow the Scottish book of 1929[1] and announce "The Canadian Liturgy, etc." was considered too radical a change, but the title "Holy Eucharist" was accepted as an alternative to "Holy Communion."

General Rubrics (p. 66)

Distinct from rubrics governing the performance of the rite, there was seen to be a need for a statement about the circumstances of its performance and the lives of the participants. This perception resulted in the establishment of four criteria: there should be frequent communion, material support for the maintenance of worship and evangelism, the intent to uphold the integrity and unity of the Body of Christ, and recognition of the corporate nature of worship. The rubric dealing with the first of these, frequency of communion, was simply patterned after the South African Prayer Book. The rubric dealing with personal lifestyle, however, occasioned great difficulty, as a balance was sought between ineffective piety and moral absolutism.

Title (p. 67)

In 1952 the 1918 title of the service had been left standing before the General Rubrics, when these had been separated

---

1. References to contemporary Anglican Liturgies cited here are taken from Bernard Wigan, The Liturgy in English (London: Oxford University Press, 1962).

from the ones specific to the performance of the rite. Between the two sets of rubrics had been inserted the caption "The Service." It was a signal, at the very outset, of the distinctiveness of the 1952 rite, but subsequently, it disappeared when a separate title page was chosen and the 1918 title of the service was restored.

Opening Rubrics (p. 67)

The origin of these is the second rubric on p. 265 of the 1918 book. It was agreed in these rubrics to specify the Table as the "Lord's," and not to specify where the priest should locate himself at it. The Rubrics Committee, headed by Dean A. Riley of St. James' Cathedral, Toronto, also deleted references to the location of the Table. Virtually all altars at this time were fixed on the "east" wall of the sanctuary; so the deletion of location allowed for the nave altars that were beginning to appear in Liturgical Movement parishes for the new "Parish Communion." The first and third of these rubrics are derived from a rubric similarly placed in the South African (1929) rite.

The Introit and Opening Prayers (p. 67)

Since its separation from the Morning Office and Litany, the Anglican liturgy had had an unsatisfactory beginning; the need for a rubric ordering the priest to say audibly the Lord's Prayer and the Collect for Purity is an indication of this. Whether seen by the priest as the continuation of his own preparation in the sacristy or as a preparation for worship done by all, the act tended to be individualistic in style and to lack the rallying force indicative of the start of a corporate event. Hallam and Palmer in their questionnaire had raised the point of whether or not the eucharist, like the daily offices, should have "opening sentences." Initially rejected, the matter surfaced again when the choice of a traditional wording for the Peace left a scriptural alternative (Philippians 1:2) without a place. Unwilling to let go, the revisers inserted the Philippians text as a greeting between priest and people with which to commence the service. Its merits apart, the Greeting was criticized as one of the elements setting the Canadian liturgy of

1952 apart from others in the Communion; and this, along with a desire to include psalmody, led to its replacement by the provision for entrance psalms in the mode proper to Western liturgies (although these were optional and generally replaced by an entrance hymn). The prayers followed unchanged.

The Commandments (pp. 68–70)

In the 1962 Prayer Book, this section of the Preparation consists of three elements: the Decalogue, Christ's Summary of the Law, and the Kyrie. The Decalogue had been shortened in 1952 by trimming the second, fourth, and tenth commandments of their commentary, and the 1918 requirement reversed by requiring these commandments to be read only once a month and on great festivals. This was already common practice in Canada, and in accordance with general liturgical thought throughout the Anglican Communion. Carrington (who had joined Palmer in a vain attempt to have the first commandment drawn from Exodus with its reference to the deliverance from Egypt) wrote in his memorandum that these were Hebrew liturgical texts which had passed directly into the apostolic church as fundamental formulas recollecting the first Covenant, and thus, should be kept in full with their Hebrew character emphasized. The Commandments were subsequently restored in their entirety (with permission to omit the commentary in numbers two and four), but the difficulty of their length remained and the rubric allowed their use to be minimized.

The 1952 addition to the Decalogue of an "eleventh commandment" was a unique and distinctive feature of the Canadian rite:

> Hear also what our Lord Jesus Christ saith: A new commandment I give unto you That ye love one another; as I have loved you, that ye also love one another.

Regarded popularly as an oddity, and professionally as a liturgical anomaly, this addition was removed and used later as an Offertory sentence for Maundy Thursday.

The Summary of the Law was considered extensively[1] and in the end adopted in a form which made clear its origin in the Hebrew Shemah, a form found in the Scottish Prayer Book and copied extensively.

The introduction of the Kyrie to the 1952 rite was a restoration to its customary place and form suggested by the questionnaire. The words are those of 1549, later adopted by the Scottish, South African, and American 1928 Prayer Books, but only in Canada was it treated as an optional addition to the Decalogue or Summary.

The Collects (p. 70) *Collects reintroduced in the 1952 rite*

The traditional greeting between priest and people, dropped from 1552 and its heirs, had been restored in almost all revisions and, as suggested in the questionnaire, was reintroduced in the 1952 rite.

The 1918 book, like its predecessors, ordered a common collect for church and state to be said before the Collect of the Day. Since the intention of this prayer was repeated in the Intercession, it was agreed to make its use optional (to satisfy some who felt strongly about its retention) and the first of the 1918 collects was provided.

The option of multiple collects was raised in the questionnaire, but with the possible exception of the Collect for Church and State, the revisers were agreed from the first on a single prayer to set the theme for the day.

The Bible Readings (pp. 70–71)

There were three principal changes in this section: the provision for other readers than the priest; the official recognition, in the rubric before the Gospel, of the role of the deacon; and the inclusion of a Gradual, which might be chosen from the Table of Psalms provided. The response after the Gospel was changed following the publication of the 1952 rite, so as to accord with the English 1928, American 1928, Ceylon, Bombay, and Indian 1960 usages in directing praise specifically

---

1. Blott, *op. cit.*, p.99f.

to the incarnate Word. Failure to include an Old Testament lesson was not due to opposition among the revisers, but rather to their reliance for the selection of readings on Carrington, who simply adopted a current English proposal which had only epistles and gospels.

Response to the Readings — Creed and Sermon (p. 71f)

In dealing with the Creed, the Canadian revisers were greatly influenced by the thinking of Bishop John Dowden as reported in a recently released American study book on the eucharist:[1] making changes, for example, in the punctuation of the second paragraph of the Creed describing the divine nature of Christ (from "God of God" to "God, of God"); and adopting the Scottish wording at the beginning of the third paragraph describing the Holy Spirit as Lord independently of its function as "The Giver of Life." The Canadians also followed the American recommendation in changing the preposition in the clause describing Christ's work in creating from "By" to "Through," and in requiring the use of the Creed on Sundays and Holy Days only, as the Prayer Books of England 1928, Ceylon, India, and Japan had also done. The word *holy*, inexplicably omitted from the 1549 translation of the Creed, was also restored to the description of the church.

In the 1952 rite, Canada followed the lead of England 1928, South Africa, and Ceylon in making the Sermon optional. Prayer Book Studies IV, however, published the next year, had concluded that "the Sermon has a place within the Liturgy by right,"[2] and the Canadian revisers subsequently agreed that it should be assumed a sermon would be preached at the eucharist, although no rubric specifically ordered it.

The Offertory (pp. 71–74)

The four eucharistic acts begin with the Offertory; and here the Canadian revisers made a number of changes designed to emphasize the fact that worshippers were identifying with

1. *Prayer Book Studies IV, The Eucharistic Liturgy (New York, 1952).*
2. *Ibid. p.187.*

Christ's acts of taking bread and wine so that, with him, they could offer their lives to God.

The first change concerned the Offertory Sentences. The offering made at this point was, in Cranmer's mind, simply a collection of money to be used for the work of the church. Hence, sentences were chosen with a view to encouraging generosity. Unfortunately, however, many of them could be interpreted in a manner that suggested the mechanical buying of God's favour and had become little used. In the 1952 rite, as recommended in a Report by Clark, those that seemed most mercenary were weeded out, and the remaining collection was headed by two sentences that clearly established the note of self-offering connected with the offering of the bread and wine.[1] The first of these is found in a number of revisions since 1662. The second is uniquely Canadian, introduced in 1918, but now moved to a place of prominence. After publication of the 1955 draft book, further deletions and additions strengthened this theology of the Offertory, and in addition, some sentences were regrouped for seasonal use.

The note of self-offering connected with the bread and wine was further emphasized in the rubrics which governed the Offertory. In 1549 the priest had been ordered to set the bread and wine upon the altar, but in 1552 all reference to the elements was removed at this point; and when this rubric was restored in 1662, the priest was simply ordered to "place" the bread and wine upon the Table. In other revisions, amplification of the rubric at this point had raised difficult questions; so Hallam and Palmer simply suggested that the oblations be treated as were the alms: that the priest "present and place" them on the altar.

A significant addition to the rubric, which arose directly out of the criticism of the 1952 rite, was the provision for an Offertory Procession. There was precedent for this in the Indian and Japanese Prayer Books, but its main impetus was the customary usage in parishes associated with the Liturgical Movement.

---

1. Colin Buchanan, The End of the Offertory — An Anglican Study (Bramcote, 1978) pp.19-33, makes clear the degree of change effected here.

Like the Introits and Graduals, it was an option not widely used, being a genre of liturgy only just coming to birth in Canada and from which the 1962 rite was essentially different. The last of the changes designed to restore the emphasis on the Offertory was the provision of a blessing that could be said over the alms and oblations. This blessing, similar to that in the Scottish Prayer Book, was chosen in preference to Carrington's suggestion of an Offertory prayer, which the new medium of television had "popularized" at the time of the coronation of Queen Elizabeth II. It is a quotation of parts of the blessing spoken by King David over the free-will offerings of the people of Israel for the Temple.

The Intercession (p. 7)

As with the lessons, here too rubrical direction was changed to allow for other clergy to share with the celebrant in doing the liturgy.[1]

The Hallam-Palmer questionnaire had suggested the possibility of a series of biddings prefacing the "Prayer for the Church," and four were added in 1952, concluding with the Cranmerian "Let us pray for the whole state of Christ's Church militant here in earth." Only the first or last bidding had to be used, but their order anticipates the contents of the Intercession; and with the provision for "one or more others if so desired" and periods of silent prayer between each of them, there is the potential of rendering the prayer itself redundant. This occurrence seems too apt to be accidental; however, its possibility is not recognized in the rubric governing the Intercession itself which "shall" be said. These revisers were careful to distinguish between "shall" and "may" in rubrical directions. The Biddings are unique to the Canadian book.

Within the prayer itself, the section dealing with the state was broadened to include all nations and their rulers, Chris-

---

1. *For most congregations at this time the priest was the minister and did all the parts himself. The few Anglo-Catholic parishes that had "High Mass," using a number and variety of ministers, were oddities. Some sound churchmen might not want to be bothered even with what one referred to as "little boys in red cassocks scuttling about the sanctuary."*

tian or otherwise, and the reference to the Privy Council replaced by "all that are put in authority" under the monarch. The duty of such is no longer to punish wickedness and vice, but only to administer justice and maintain "thy true religion and virtue." The removal of the comma after "religion" equated religion and virtue in a way 1662 had not.

Chaplains returning from World War I had pointed out to the 1918 revisers the pastoral necessity of including the departed in the Intercession; and failure to do so again in 1952, after a second World War, had been strongly criticized. Palmer's suggestion, a bare remembrance of the departed and a commemoration of the worthy (his specific reference to "thy saints" was removed by the Committee) was incorporated into 1962 to fill this need. It is interesting to note, however, that in this matter, whereas England 1928, Scotland, Ceylon, India, and Japan all followed the precedent of the Scottish book of 1637 in restoring Prayers for the Departed and a Commemoration of Saints, the Canadians did not, nor in this case were they influenced by Prayer Book Studies IV.

The Doxology, added at the end of the Intercession in 1952, followed a precedent set by the English 1928 book only. The revisers wanted to give recognition to the importance of this prayer, but doing so by this means simply compounded the confusion of the liturgical pattern at this point in Anglican liturgies of the 1552 model, to which Carrington had alluded in his memorandum.[1]

The Act of Confession (p. 76)

This section consists of the Invitation, Confession, Absolution, and Comfortable Words, all done in 1662 by the celebrating priest, with the exception of the Confession which could be led or said, on behalf of the people, by "one of the Ministers." Subsequent to 1952, the Canadian revisers changed the rubrics to allow the Invitation to be done by "one

---

1. Blott, op. cit., Appendix B, p.2, Offertory. "It is worth noting," Carrington observes, "that, if ancient liturgical precedent is to be considered, the Offertory should come after the Church Militant prayer." Without the doxology the Intercession could at a stretch be considered part of the Offertory.

of the Ministers" and to have the Confession said by "both Priest and people humbly kneeling." (The "Minister" must have been lay.) The Absolution and Comfortable Words remained priestly matters.

Significant changes were made in the wording of the Invitation and Confession themselves. By extending the Invitation to those who intended to lead "the" new life (rather than the indefinite "a"), the Canadian revisers brought in a valuable link between the eucharist and the new life to which God raised Jesus.[1]

The questionnaire had suggested deleting from the Confession the minatory phrase, "Provoking most justly thy wrath and indignation against us." This suggestion was adopted in 1952, as was the suggestion to remove a reference to the intolerable burden sin placed on man. In this, the Canadian followed the sole example of the recently published liturgy of Ceylon, and efforts, after publication of the 1955 draft book, to restore the excised phrases came to nothing. For Canadians, as for other victors in war, the 1950s were still a time of exulting over two victories in two World Wars. Few, if any, Anglicans saw the irony in softening the Confession.

Carrington had been asked to suggest changes in the Comfortable Words, but his own feeling was that these sentences as they stood represented the evangelical element in the eucharist at its best, and no action was taken beyond substituting "labour" for "travail" in the first, and changing the conjunction "so" in the second to an adverb by making it the second word in the sentence.

---

1. Cf. *The Anthems For Easter Day, BCP, Canada, 1962, p.182.*

13 Thanksgiving and consecration

The Title (p. 78)
In 1662 the central prayer of the canon had been designated "the Prayer of Consecration." This was a laudable attempt to identify one of the basic acts of the eucharist (the blessing of the bread and wine), but it orphaned the preceding dialogue, Preface, and Sanctus which were also parts of the same act.[1] In 1952 this was corrected by placing a title in the rubric before the dialogue.

"After which the Priest shall proceed with THE THANKSGIVING."

In 1962, after the example of the Scottish Liturgy, English 1928, South African, Ceylonese, Indian, and Bombay, the title was set out from the rubric.

"the Priest shall then proceed with the holy Eucharist in THANKSGIVING and CONSECRATION"

Reference to the "holy Eucharist" at this point reflected the perception by some of the revisers that the term applied to this section of the liturgy only.

The Opening Dialogue (p. 78)
By ancient custom, the Canon began with a dialogue between celebrant and congregation. After completing the action of the Offertory, the priest rallied the people for the next step

1. G. A. Michell, Landmarks in Liturgy (London, 1961) p.59. Cf. also F. L. Cross, ed., The Oxford Dictionary of the Christian Church (London, 1957) p.228. The designation in 1662 was, however, consistent with current thought which identified the Te igitur in the Roman rite as the beginning of the Canon.

DAVID 3IER STUDIOS, MONTREAL

"Praise God from whom all blessings flow...." Archbishop Howard Clark and the Rev. Dr. Ramsey Armitage are seen here with a copy of the revised Prayer Book which, after sixteen years of work, was passed by General Synod in 1959. There was a real sense that this was what the church wanted.

ANGLICAN CHURCH OF CANADA

The 1962 Prayer Book represented a "concensus fidelium"— a codification of the generally accepted beliefs and customs of Anglicans in Canada in the first part of the twentieth century. Seen here with the book at the 1959 General Synod are (L to R) Archdeacon Cosgrave of Trinity College whose deft adaptation of Coverdale's language in the Psalter won great praise, Archbishop Carrington, Archbishop Clark, Ramsey Armitage, Principal of Wycliffe College, and Fr. Palmer, S.S.J.E. Armitage and Palmer were trusted representatives respectively of the Evangelical and Catholic elements in the church. They always sat side by side at Committee meetings and formed a close relationship.

with the exclaimer: "The Lord be with you," to which they responded: "And with thy spirit." This greeting had been included in the liturgy of 1549, which kept to the traditional order, but was omitted from 1552 since, presumably, those who were to give thanks had been addressed in the Invitation preceding the Confession and, as requested, had drawn near. Although the Anglican Church did not adopt the theology or ceremony of 1552, it did, for the most part in 1662, adopt its form. Thus the greeting remained absent although the rationale behind its absence was gone.

Hallam and Palmer in the questionnaire asked the Committee whether the mutual salutation should be returned (as in practice it sometimes was) or whether, instead, the Peace should be inserted here. The first reaction at North Hatley was to restore the traditional greeting. After some consideration, however, the revisers decided to replace it with the traditional form of the Peace, but to make this exchange of the peace the final act of that segment of the rite which begins with the Offertory and goes on to include the Comfortable Words. The rite was printed this way in 1951, but at the final review in 1952, the Peace was made the opening exchange in the dialogue initiating the Thanksgiving and Consecration.

In wording, this Canadian version of the Peace was slightly different from that used in other Anglican rites, but its position made it unique. The only parallel is that of the Bombay liturgy, which begins the dialogue with a Trinitarian invocation of God's grace upon the congregation.

Along with the related greeting at the beginning of the 1952 synaxis, Carrington felt this positioning of the Peace should be "objectively reconsidered," his own preference being to restore "The Lord be with you" to the dialogue and the Peace to its traditional Western position at the end of the canon. In the 1962 rite this was done.

The Preface (p. 78)

Noting that in earlier times the Preface had been the opening statement of the Canon, blessing God for his mighty acts in creation and history, Carrington's memorandum recommended an optional "Special Preface" for any Sunday, along the lines of the second and third clauses of the General Thanksgiving. As only the liturgies of England 1928, Ceylon, and South Africa had proper Sunday Prefaces and these did not fulfill the function referred to by Carrington, there was little impetus in this direction. When action was finally taken, it was in the form of a compromise, avoiding a Proper Preface, but adding the words "Creator and Preserver of all things" to the exisiting preface.

The Proper Prefaces   (p. 79f)

The majority of the work here was done in connection with the 1952 rite on the basis of a report prepared by Palmer. Along with new content, it introduced the concepts of octaves and eves.[1]

The use of the Christmas Preface was extended to include the Annunciation by placing the particularizing phrase "as at this time" in italics, to indicate it could be omitted. A Preface was added from the American 1928 book for use from New Year's Day to Epiphany Eve, and on the feasts of the Purification and Transfiguration. The Preface for Passion Sunday until Maundy Thursday inclusive, was an extract taken by Palmer from the first Exhortation in the 1549 book, and is uniquely Canadian. The use of the Easter Preface was extended from seven days to Ascension Eve inclusive, and also to Memorial Services. The use of the Preface for the Ascension was lengthened from seven days to Whitsun Eve inclusive. The Whitsunday Preface, modified according to the American 1928 usage by deleting reference to the wind and fiery tongue mentioned in Acts, was also to be used at ordinations and synods, so facilitated by again italicizing the phrase "as at this time." The Trinity Preface is, apparently, Palmer's recension of

---

1. *The Christian Church adapted the Jewish day which ran from sunset to sunset. Thus, for example, the Feast of All Saints would begin not on the morning of November 1, but at sunset on October 31, All Hallows Eve. "Octave" referred to the eighth day after a feast reckoning inclusively and therefore always falling on the same day of the week as the Feast. Cf. Cross, op. cit., p. 974.*

one found in the Scottish Liturgy, English 1928, American 1928, South African, Ceylonese, Indian, and Irish. And finally, the Preface for All Saints' Day and other Festivals of Saints is one found in both the Scottish and American 1928 liturgies, based on Hebrews 12:1 and I Peter 5:4.

The Benedictus Qui Venit (p. 81)

A common feature of almost all the revised liturgies of the Anglican Communion was the restoration of the "Benedictus," removed in 1552 on the grounds that it might support the doctrine of the corporeal presence of Christ in the sacrament. Carrington's attempt to restore it to the 1952 revision had been decisively defeated, even though the Benedictus had never really gone out of use, having been retained in Merbecke's musical setting of the service. It was restored to the 1962 rite as an option, but a note in the minutes of the Committee to the effect that the words apply to the whole liturgy, indicated the continuing apprehension of some churchmen. Following a recommendation in Prayer Book Studies IV, its use was allowed either following the Sanctus or immediately before Communion.

The Sanctus (pp. 79 & 81)

The Sanctus, in its Anglican version, remained unchanged and, as before, was printed with the second half of the Preface both before and after the Proper Prefaces.

The Prayer of Consecration (p. 82f)

Revision of the Prayer of Consecration had been the major task of the Committee preparing the 1952 rite. The lack of any change here had been the chief complaint of many critics after the first revision of 1918. The 1662 prayer, they said, did not establish at the start a proper note of praise, and was not inclusive enough to represent the thinking of the early church.

Consequently, across the Anglican Church of Canada, there were many areas where it had long been the custom to add the "Prayer of Oblation" (the first of the two post-communion prayers following the Lord's Prayer in the 1918 book) to the Prayer of Consecration and, in some instances, to follow both with the Lord's Prayer. Essentially, however, this had always been an *ad hoc* measure. So, in addition to proposals for allowing the use of the American or Scottish prayers, there had been submissions to the Revision Committee of models, based on the Scottish Canon, for a proper Canadian Prayer of Consecration: from the Diocese of Ottawa in 1918, an *anamnesis* to be inserted before the "Prayer of Oblation"; from Bishop Bidwell of Ontario in 1921, an *anamnesis* and *epiclesis* to replace the "Prayer of Oblation"; and from the Diocese of Algoma in 1935, an *anamnesis* and general invocation of the Spirit to be inserted before the "Prayer of Oblation," which prayer was commonly accepted as a proper oblation of the elements.

The 1952 Prayer of Consecration

To answer the first criticism of the 1662 Prayer, Hallam and Palmer made two suggestions. The first was to begin the prayer with the introductory phrase used in both the English and American liturgies of 1928: "All glory be to thee." An alternative suggestion was to begin with the phrase "Blessing and glory and thanksgiving be unto thee," which appears to be an adaptation of an act of praise from the Book of Revelation (7:12) and to have originated in the joint work of Hallam and Palmer on the questionnaire. The Committee's choice of the second phrase clearly established the note of praise, and gave the 1952 prayer a distinctly Canadian introduction.

Other changes made at this time to the 1662 prayer were the addition of the Incarnation to the recital of God's saving acts, using a phrase from the South African rite — "to take our nature upon him" — and, in the institution narrative, the change of "Testament" to "Covenant."

The criticism that the 1662 prayer was not inclusive enough could be met by the addition of a new paragraph containing the traditional elements which had been omitted: an *anamnesis* (the commemoration of the Passion, Resurrection, and Ascension of Christ), an oblation (offering to the Father the bread and wine of Christ's sacrifice), an *epeclesis* (invoking the

Cranmer opposed - how can one offer to God?

[handwritten annotation: & send the Holy Spirit upon the community]

Father to send the Holy Spirit upon the bread and wine that they might be the body and blood of Christ), and a doxology. The simplest way of doing this, and the one most commonly recommended, was to add the "Prayer of Oblation" to the Prayer of Consecration by the use of the conjunctive "Wherefore." Hallam and Palmer dutifully presented this option to the Committee, but did not consider it a sound choice.

The first of the choices presented in the questionnaire was a paragraph compiled by Hallam and Palmer together. It consisted of a brief address, standard to most revisions and formed by placing "Wherefore" before the opening phrase of the "Prayer of Oblation." This was followed by an intention, unique to Canada and similar to that in the *Unde et memores* of the Roman rite. Then followed an *anamnesis*, an offering of praise, and the Doxology from the 1662 "Prayer of Oblation." With a few minor changes in wording, this suggestion was adopted for the 1952 rite:

> Wherefore, O Lord and heavenly Father, in union with all thy holy Church, we do this in remembrance of him who died, and rose again, and ever liveth to make intercession for us, presenting unto thy divine Majesty this our thankoffering and service, through the merits and mediation of thy beloved Son, Jesus Christ our Lord, by whom, and with whom, in the unity of the Holy Spirit, all honour and glory be unto thee, O Father Almighty, world without end. Amen.[1]

Later, in the light of criticism of the new paragraph, both Hallam and Palmer set to work again. Hallam re-drafted the third paragraph, staying as close as possible to the 1952 *anamnesis*, but adding an oblation:

> and we present before thy Divine Majesty these thy holy gifts of bread and wine; entirely desiring thy fatherly goodness to accept

---

1. Blott, *op. cit.*, *Appendix C, Report Of The Committee On Revision Of The Common Book Of Payer*, The Order For The Administration of The Lord's Supper Or Holy Communion, *p. 9*.

this sacrifice of praise and thanksgiving; and we humbly beseech thee to grant." [Here the draft ended.][1]

Palmer, traveling about the province of British Columbia, and attendant to the long-standing desires of the church there, returned to the concept he had put to Hallam when the two began work on the questionnaire: "I think that the more of the Prayer of Oblation which we place after the Consecration the more we shall meet the wishes of the Province of British Colombia and many other churchmen of various schools of thought."[2]

The committee, meanwhile, had before it Carrington's memorandum, which gave the Prayer of Consecration careful treatment. He began by delineating the two Anglican traditions: that of 1549, from which came the Prayer in the liturgies of Scotland, America, South Africa, and others; and that of 1552, which was the source of current English, Irish, Canadian, Australian, and New Zealand prayers.[3] The basic question was whether Canada should change from the 1552 model to that of 1549.

The 1962 Prayer of Consecration

The first two paragraphs of the prayer from the 1952 rite were left unchanged, and a new third paragraph was produced by Archbishop Clark and a committee consisting of Dean Riley, Father Palmer, Mr. R.A. Baldwin, and The Reverend Dr. Ramsey Armitage. This paragraph represents the best work of the revisers and was approved both by Hallam for its theology and Armitage for the beauty of its wording. It appeared in the 1955 draft book and won general approval, but had to be re-

---

1. *Draft of the third paragraph in Hallam's hand. Armitage Papers, Wycliffe College, Toronto.*
2. *The Reverend Roland F. Palmer, Letter to the Right Reverend W.T. Hallam on the subject of reaction to the 1952 rite, dated August 1, 1954, Armitage Papers. On April 20, 1950, Palmer had sent Hallam a proposal consisting of the anamnesis and oblation from the Scottish Liturgy with at doxology based on the last sentence of the 1918 Bidding Prayer.*
3. *Blott op. cit. Appendix B, p.3f.*

worked when criticism of the oblation aroused fears that some Low Churchmen might repudiate the book on that account.[1]

An Analysis of the Third Paragraph

1955 TEXT	SOURCE	1962 TEXT	SOURCE
	Canadian Address		
Wherefore, O Lord and Heavenly Father	Scot., Am. 1928, Eng.1928, S. Africa, India	*Wherefore, O Father, Lord of Heaven and earth*	
	Intention		
In union with all thy holy church	Roman rite- *Unde et memores,* "together with thy holy people" cf. II Pet. 2:9	*we thy humble servants with all thy holy Church*	*Unde et memores*

All the Anglican Revisions state the intention of doing what Christ commanded in the Institution, usually having some form of the Scottish formula: "according to the institution of thy dearly beloved son ... we ... make ... the memorial thy son hath commanded ..." The Canadian rite alone adds the intention of acting with the whole church.

	Anamnesis		
we thy humble servants remember before thee the blessed passion and precious death, the mighty resurrection and glorious ascension of thy beloved son;	Scot., Am. 1928, Eng. 1928, S. African, Ceylon, Ind., Jap., P.B. Studies IV	*remembering the precious death of thy beloved Son, his mighty resurrection, and glorious ascension, and looking for his coming again in glory,*	Can. omits "Blessed Passion" In Can. alone the eschatological reference stands between the anamnesis and a second statement of intention.

1. Blott op. cit., p.113, fn. 338.

Only Scotland and India have the eschatological associated with the *anamnesis*.

1955 TEXT	SOURCE	1962 TEXT	SOURCE
	Oblation		
And looking for his coming (in power and great glory) we present unto thy divine Majesty this holy Bread of eternal life and cup of everlasting salvation;	S. African and Jap. associated the eschatological hope with oblation. Carrington memorandum. Cf. Eng. 1928 "set forth before thy Divine Majesty" S. African, Roman rite, *Unde et Memores* - "*panem sanctum vitae aeternae, et Calicem salutis perpetuae*"		

Second Intention

		do make before thee, in this sacrament of the holy Bread of eternal life and Cup of ever-lasting salvation, the memorial which he hath commanded;	Cf. Diocese of Ottawa 1918 proposal S. Africa, *Unde et memores*

Ottawa 1918: "do we celebrate and make here before thy Divine Majesty with these Thy Holy gifts, the memorial Thy Son hath willed us to make...." This is the Scottish oblation without the operative phrase referring to the Holy gifts: "which we now offer unto thee." The 1962 rite also omits the operative phrase, and substitutes the words "in this sacrament of ... everlasting salvation," for "with these Thy Holy gifts." This section now becomes an extended form of the Intention (found in all the other Anglican revisions) of making "the memorial thy Son hath commanded." Its placement after the *anamnesis* is similar to England 1928, Ceylon, and Japan. The oblation of the elements has been removed.

1955 TEXT	SOURCE	1962 TEXT	SOURCE
	Supplication		
and we entirely desire ... benefits of his passion	1662 "Prayer of Oblation"	*Unchanged from the 1955 text.*	
	Epiclesis		
and we pray	Cf. South African, "<u>and we</u> humbly beseech thee to pour the Holy Spirit upon us and upon these gifts, that	*and we pray*	
that by the inspiration of thy Holy Spirit		*that*	
		by the power of thy Holy Spirit	
all we who are partakers of this holy commun-ion, may	<u>all we who are partakers in this holy Communion may</u> worthily receive the most precious Body and Blood of thy Son, and	*all we who are partakers of this holy Commun-ion may*	
be fulfilled with thy grace and heavenly benediction	<u>be fulfilled with the grace and heavenly benediction</u>"	*be fulfilled with thy grace and heavenly benediction*	

121

The underlined sections of South Africa, with the added phrase "by the inspiration of thy Holy Spirit" inserted after "that," form the original 1955 *epiclesis*. The change of wording in the phrase may have been intended to strengthen this section of the prayer. Scotland, Ceylon, and Bombay refer to the "life-giving power" of the Holy Spirit coming upon the oblations that "they may become the Body and Blood of thy most dearly beloved Son." Carrington, however, regarded the *epiclesis* as a retrogressive fourth-century introduction, and Palmer took the generally accepted position that the words of Institution were the central and essential moment of the prayer. This element, therefore, remained in an embryonic stage.

1955 TEXT	SOURCE	1962 TEXT	SOURCE
through Jesus Christ … the Holy Spirit … world without end.	1662 "Prayer of Oblation" with the change of "Ghost" to "Spirit"	*Unchanged from the 1955 text.*	

	Acclamation		
<u>And here all the people shall say or sing</u>: Amen.	Canadian wording, but setting the acclamation apart is English 1928.	<u>And all the people shall answer</u>: Amen.	English 1928

Of the two Anglican traditions delineated by Carrington, the 1955 Prayer of Consecration was of the 1549 model. The subsequent alterations in the text changed this, however, and the final version was clearly 1552 in type.

The Silence (p. 83)

In the 1952 rite the rubric after the Prayer of Consecration ordered the priest to kneel at the altar and observe a short period of silence. Traditionally, at the end of the Canon, there had been a pause for the fraction, which was accompanied by private devotions. The Anglican rite included the fraction within the Canon, but the silence had been restored at its conclusion in the rites of Scotland, South Africa, and Ceylon. Dropped in 1955, the silence was restored in 1962 as a prelude to the

Peace, the priest remaining standing. This device allowed those priests who wished to do so to break the bread as ordered within the prayer and to break it again at the traditional place.

The Peace (p. 83)

Considered initially as the final act of Offertory, but in 1952 made the opening statement of the Thanksgiving and Consecration dialogue, the Peace was restored in 1962 to its customary position in mediaeval rites. The form was that adopted by the rites of Ceylon, India, and Japan.

The Prayer of Humble Access (p. 83)

A noticeable change was the removal in 1952 of this prayer from between the Sanctus and the Prayer of Consecration to a place before the Communion, where it was to be said by all rather than the priest alone. This corresponded to the way in which the prayer had been used in 1549, and to the current usage of Scotland, American 1928, South Africa, and Ceylon.

The Communion (p. 84)

This title was introduced in 1955 as a capitalized section of the rubric preceding the Prayer of Humble Access. Its placement after that prayer in 1962 is an oddity which seems to make the Payer of Humble Access a part of the Thanksgiving and Consecration, rather than the communion devotion which its rubric indicates.

The Words of Administration (p. 84)

These remained unchanged, but the rubric governing their use was changed in 1952, so as not to require the whole sentence to be said to each communicant.

The Agnus Dei (p. 84)

As Carrington foresaw, his strong recommendation of the Benedictus Qui Venit raised the issue of including the Agnus Dei which, like the Benedictus, had been removed from the 1552 Prayer Book but included in Merbecke's music for the liturgy.[1] The Agnus Dei was restored in 1962, but as an example of the sort of hymns or anthems which might be used "In the Communion Time." The rites of Scotland, Japan, Ceylon, and India restore it as a pre-communion devotion, but only that of Bombay treats it like the Canadian rite, as a hymn to be sung during communion. The Canadian text, like that of the Indian, has the singular "sin" rather than the usual "takest away the sins of the world," wishing in this way to portray Christ's atonement as a once-for-all act of redemption rather than an antidote for circumstantial misdeeds of individuals.

The Supplementary Consecration (p. 84)

If, during communion, more of either element was needed, the priest was instructed, in the 1662 rite, to repeat the relevant clause from the institution narrative in the Prayer of Consecration. What this appeared to imply about the theology of consecration — that consecration of the elements was accomplished by the recital of some sacred words — was unfortunate, to say the least. In the Canadian revision the rubrics committee, headed by Dean Riley, prefaced the relevant words of Institution with a supplication which clearly set this act within the whole context of Thanksgiving and Consecration.

The Ablutions

After the communion of the people, the 1662 book had ordered that any of the consecrated elements remaining be placed on the altar and covered with a fair linen cloth. A second rubric ordered the priest to proceed with the Lord's Prayer. High Churchmen wanted either to reserve the sacrament properly or to take the ablutions at that point (as, indeed, many clergy did). Leaving the consecrated elements on the altar, while going on with the service, created devotional problems, given their High Church theology of the Real Presence. In 1962 the first direction was removed and a rubric was placed after the Blessing, which allowed the ablutions to be done then or immediately after the communion of the people. Any practical problem caused by a hiatus in the liturgy would, however,

---

1. *Blott, op. cit., Appendix B, p.3.*

not be resolved by transferring the act from one point to another.

Post Communion

The ambivalence of the Canadian church reflected in the matter of the ablutions is apparent throughout the immediate post-communion section of the liturgy. All the other revisions which make use of titles to identify sections of the service have one at this point, such as "The Thanksgiving" or "Thanksgiving after Communion." The failure of the Canadian revisers to include a title here was connected with the contentious issue of what place the Lord's Prayer was to have.

The Lord's Prayer

After 1549 Cranmer had removed the Our Father from its traditional place at the end of the consecration and placed it immediately after the receiving of communion, where its address and petitions perfectly suited his sacramental theology as expressed in 1552. According to this theology, the purpose of what later was named the Prayer of Consecration was to set forth Jesus' precious death and stir up the spirit of each worshipper, so that he or she might go in heart and mind to the Upper Room and, in the act of taking bread and wine, be one in spirit with the Spirit of Christ.[1] In this context, nothing could be more fitting than to address the Father with the very words Christ had taught his followers to pray. To insert a title ("Thanksgiving after Communion") would remove the Lord's Prayer from this intense and mystical role in the act of com-

---

1. Cf. Hague, above, p. 31. Charles Neil and J. M. Willoughby, eds., The Tutorial Prayer Book (London, 1963) p. 273f. in discussing the black rubric, conclude: "The true spiritual presence of Christ is his presence by his Spirit, to our spirits...." Colin Buchanan, What Did Cranmer Think He Was Doing? (Bramcote, Notts, 1976) p. 2f., argues that there must be a common understanding of Cranmer's thinking about both sacraments, baptism and communion. In baptism there is nothing "in" or "under" the water, rather the Holy Spirit works through the administration of the sacrament. Likewise there is nothing "in" or "under" the bread; God works through the administration of it. "The whole comparison with baptism," Buchanan writes, "entailed a communicating of grace by the Spirit to the recipients. The whole locus of this communicating was the point of reception, but a true communicating it was."

munion by placing it in another context. To transfer the prayer to its place after the Prayer of Consecration would not only do the same, but (following the same line of thinking about its use) would imply an objective Presence in the elements antithetical to this theology. The failure of 1952 to restore the payer to its customary place was a notable factor in making this rite exceptional among revised Anglican liturgies, and strong recommendations for such a restoration followed. Among the revisers, however, only Palmer pressed the point. Carrington had reservations about it; and by omitting a title for this section, the prayer could be interpreted either in the manner of 1552 or as the first act of thanksgiving after communion, as many had done since 1662. Theological fitness, the precedent of every current Anglican revision, and the desire of a large part of the Canadian church, all were to no avail: the Prayer Book of 1962 retained the Lord's Prayer in its 1552 position.

The Prayer of Thanksgiving (p. 85)

This prayer had come into the 1662 rite unchanged from 1552, and had continued to be used with little, if any, change in its various revisions since then. The 1952 rite left it unchanged as well, but significant alterations appeared in 1962. In formulating models for a new third paragraph for the Prayer of Consecration, Carrington had begun with the assumption that the element of self-oblation in the old "Prayer of Oblation" should be transferred to the Prayer of Thanksgiving after communion. This device originated in the draft Prayer Book proposed by a group of English clergy in 1923.[1] He consequently drew up a model of such a prayer in his first memorandum. The Canadian revisers

---

(Note 1, continued from page 125) *Chadwick, op. cit., pp. 114-129, paints a sympathetic portrait of Cranmer as a man whose spiritual perceptions fitted but awkwardly the molds presented to him by contemporary theology. Cf. also Dix, op. cit., pp. 640-674, and Richard F.* Buxton, Eucharist and Institution Narrative *(London, 1976) pp. 52-58.*

1. A New Prayer Book: proposals for the revision of the *Book of Common Prayer* and for additional services and prayers, drawn up by a Group of Clergy, together with a foreword by William Temple, D. Litt, Bishop of Manchester. Part I, The order of Holy Communion. I. The Office *(London, 1923) p.17.*

retained the first part of the 1662 Prayer of Thanksgiving (with a change of wording in the first clause, in order to associate the receiving of "the spiritual food" of Christ's body and blood directly with the "holy mysteries" being celebrated) but then, in a second paragraph, added the self-oblation (with the omission of the clause: "humbly beseeching thee ... heavenly benediction," phrases which had already been incorporated into the Prayer of Consecration). The effect of these changes was to give a new direction to the prayer. The 1662 prayer had been forward-looking, concluding with a petition that after the service the communicants might continue their "holy fellowship" and "do all such good works as thou has prepared for us to walk in." The orientation of 1962 was within the liturgy, its movement vertical rather than horizontal.

The Gloria In Excelsis

In 1952 the text had been amended by the omission of Cranmer's addition to the second paragraph of the petition: "Thou that takest away the sin of the world, have mercy upon us." The Scottish and American 1928 did the same; Ceylon made it optional. Some critics of 1952 wanted the Gloria at the beginning of the rite after the Commandments, but this found no support among the revisers, and Carrington had noted that its first appearance, in the *Apostolic Constitutions*, was at the end of the liturgy. Permission to omit the Gloria, allowed in 1952 on weekends in Advent and Lent, was extended to all ferial weekdays.

The Blessing

All the revisions, except Bombay and Japan, retained the Blessing introduced in 1549, and its socially interesting rubrical direction that with this the chief celebrant shall "let them depart."

The Rubrics (p. 86)

The ten rubrics following the blessing in 1662 were reduced to two. Number 6, regarding the Ablutions, was placed first, with the provision removed that had allowed the priest to have any remaining unconsecrated bread and wine for his own use. This was followed by the first 1662 rubric providing for ante-communion. The collects to be used at ante-communion followed immediately with the Lord's Prayer and the Grace to be said at the conclusion rather than at the Blessing. The second, forth, and eighth rubrics became, respectively, the last, third and first two of the 1962 general rubrics introducing the service. The fifth rubric was moved to the Offertory and altered to allow for both leavened and unleavened bread. The 1662 rubrics three, seven, and nine were no longer relevant and were omitted. The "black rubric" was removed and placed by itself at the end of the Exhortations, the clause "yet, lest the same kneeling ... be misconstrued and depraved" and the final sentence "For the Sacramental Bread ... more places than one" being replaced by paragraph three of article 28 of the Thirty-Nine Articles.

The Exhortations (p. 88f)

The final major alteration in the 1918 rite was the disposition of Exhortations — short homilies designed to instruct the people in the nature and purpose of communion, the attitude in which they ought to come to it, and the desirability of frequent reception of the sacrament. They had dropped out of general use, but were valued by many as historical documents of faith. Palmer was given the task of conflating the first two and shortening the third, and with a few changes in wording, his work was accepted. In 1962, what had been the third Exhortation was printed first. In the details of their wording, the Exhortations were peculiar to Canada; but in placing them at the end of the rite, the revisers followed a precedent set by the Scottish Liturgy, American 1928, and South Africa.

14   *Conclusion*

Thus, a liturgy for the Anglican Church of Canada grew from the seed of the letter Matthew Wilson wrote in 1896 to the Bishop of Huron. At the General Synod of 1959, two days had been set aside for the presentation and discussion of the report of the General Committee, but they were not to be needed.

H.V.R. Short, then rector of St. Barnabas' Church, St. Catharines, had studied the book with care and written a lengthy commentary on it for *His Dominion*, the journal of S.S.J.E. at Bracebridge, Ontario. He was convinced that it was "fundamentally a good effort"[1] and that prolonged debate would only result in unnecessary delay while the Committee haggled over jots and tittles. When General Synod assembled, therefore, Carrington (who in the absence of the primate was chairing the meeting) was alerted to expect a motion of acceptance from Short at the end of Clark's presentation of the General Committee's report. Carrington was glad to comply. He had previously expressed to Fr. Palmer the wish that, since the book had been accepted in principle at the last synod, a motion for acceptance of the report as presented might bring the matter to a speedy conclusion. Short, meanwhile, spoke to Clark about his plans, and enlisted the Rev. Carl Swan, rector of St. George's Church, St. Catharines, to second his motion, making it a joint effort by representatives of Trinity and Wycliffe Colleges respectively.

---

1. *The Rt. Rev. H.V.R. Short, Letter to the author on the subject of the acceptance of the report on the Prayer Book by General Synod 1959, dated Jan. 12, 1978.*

At the end of Clark's presentation, Short was on his feet. Carrington recognized him and the motion passed as delegates clapped, cheered, and sang. Clark's masterly and assured presentation had lifted members beyond the level of petty quibbling to a view of the whole accomplishment. There was a genuine sense of this being what the church wanted, and sixteen years of work, the chief of it on the eucharist, was brought to a fitting end. The ovation continued minute after minute, spontaneously ending with the words of the doxology — "Praise God from whom all blessings flow." The words were heart-felt and hopeful.

Revision of the Prayer Book in Canada grew, of course, out of the historical development of the Canadian church, and thus reflected the basic situation inherited from England: that of two theologies in unresolved conflict using the same liturgical expressions. While no specific attempt was made to resolve this conflict, the Canadian work went a long way toward redressing the balance between High and Low positions, by re-asserting the sacramental concept and the consequent position of the eucharist in the church's worship. Not much was done, however, to give better expression in the eucharist to Low Church concerns for the individual and psychological response to God — the *synaxis* was still uncertain and incomplete. As a result, Morning Prayer, which was a better *synaxis* (service of scripture reading and prayer) and generally a better piece of liturgy (by reason of such things as the active involvement of the congregation in singing and in litanies), retained its place as an alternative form of Sunday worship. A resolution to the Reformation question of how persons were to work out their salvation from day to day[1] was left to resolve itself in the daily life of the church.

More particularly, a review of the recommendations for liturgical reform proposed in England by various persons and groups from 1854 to 1876, reveals the source of the principles governing the extent and nature of the Canadian revision, and of the majority of changes as well. Carrington's plan was based

1. Cf. *above* p. 9.

solidly in these nineteenth-century proposals which, being the source of revisions made in other parts of the Anglican Communion, had the effect of bringing the Canadian liturgy into line with them.[1]

The influence of the American church was more subtle. In considering the motions put forward in 1902 by Matthew Wilson of Chatham and J.A. Worrell of Toronto, it is hard not to conclude that they must have been influenced by books such as Potter's *Memorial Papers*.[2] They wanted to make the 1662 English book fit the needs of Canada (the spirit of the Muhlenberg Memorial is certainly present, if not named). Both Shreve and Vroom, at a later date, were greatly influenced by the American revisions. Shreve's open espousal of the American example, however, provided another avenue of attack for "loyalists," and this illustrated the enigmatic position of the Canadian church, expressed well in Clark's commentary on revision:

> No Prayer Book that departed seriously from the 1662 at the Holy Communion would prove acceptable to our people. Yet the Prayer Book they are most likely to meet in their travels is that of the American Church with its Eucharist derived from the Scottish Liturgy.[3]

Turning to the Canadian church's own background, apart from its attachment to England and its proximity to the Episcopal Church, a major factor influencing revision was the violent party strife of the latter part of the nineteenth century. The threat of its revival ended work in 1905, inhibited the 1918 revision, and still intimidated churchmen both before and during the 1962 revision.

Another great influence was the size of the country. Quite apart from the preoccupation with opening, settling, and governing the land, the sheer magnitude of the distances between participants in the revision process created considerable ob-

---

1. *Cf. above p. 13f.*
2. *Alonzo Potter, ed.* The Memorial Papers *(Philadelphia, 1857).*
3. *The Most Rev. Howard H. Clark,* Prayer Book Revision in Canada, *p.12.*

stacles. In the case of the appendix, the concession to distance led to poor communication and a product of very limited vision that everybody was content to let die. The 1918 book was rushed to completion because the publisher, who had underwritten the considerable costs of travel, needed to recover his financial outlay. Even with the 1962 revision, although faster and easier travel allowed meetings in a central location, part of the cost was again borne by the publisher. And even with travel costs met, the Maritimes and British Columbia felt themselves very much on the periphery of the action.

A third factor influencing revision in Canada was the nature of the church as a voluntary society with no legal restraints. This meant that, once begun, all things were theoretically possible in revision, and therefore great care was taken to keep control of what went on. The Bible, the Prayer Book of 1662, and the Thirty-Nine Articles were reference points (to which after 1962 a very important addition would be the Solemn Declaration), but there was no "disinterested" body which could call a halt if things got out of hand, as the state could do in England. Many Canadian Anglicans did not find this freedom liberating.

Finally, an elusive but persistent factor was the influence of the "concordat," as it has been called, which is a part of the essence of Anglicanism. It was expressed well by Archbishop Clark in a letter to the clergy before what was hoped would be the final presentation to General Synod.

> May I add in conclusion a personal remark. Since our Committee began its work in 1943, there has been a remarkable charity and understanding among our members. This does not mean that we have been ready for unprincipled compromise. It does mean that we have always remembered that there are different points of view in our Church, and that it is the deliberate will of our Church that there should be room for them.[1]

These differences would have to remain so until both visions

---

1. *The Most Rev. Howard H. Clark, Letter to the Archbishops, Bishops and Clergy, The Anglican Church of Canada, Dated Feb. 20, 1957, now with the Hallam Correspondence in the General Synod Archives, Toronto.*

could, eventually, be united in one comprehensive liturgical expression.

There were, in addition, four other historical factors that helped shape revision in Canada: the fact that the work on the 1918 book was regarded as an experiment for English observers; the decision by Canadian revisers to make no change in principle or practice from 1662; the assumption that revision would not take the easier road of producing a book with alternate usages; and finally, the fact that 1962 was essentially a completion of 1918, which meant that work on the eucharist was done *de nouveau*, without benefit of a previous revision to act as a guide.

In the practical work of making revisions, the revisers had numerous sources which they could, and did, consult. The major resource, however, was the English *Book of Common Prayer*. With all its changes, the rite remained a modification of that of 1662, on which it was founded. But two other contemporary documents were fundamental as well.[1]

In the case of the 1952 rite, the Hallam-Palmer questionnaire had been formative, and for all its faults, that rite had made an important contribution to the final outcome. Of a score of significant changes proposed in 1952, three out of four remained a part of the final rite; for example, moving the long Exhortations from their interruptive place in the middle to the end, the addition of Proper Prefaces for more seasons of the liturgical year, and the presentation of the elements at the Offertory. In a similar way, the Carrington memorandum was also formative of the 1962 rite.

There is a danger of over-simplifying the facts. The questionnaire did not limit discussion to the matters it brought up; rather, at almost every point, it suggested two or three courses of action that the committee might take. So, too, in the case of

---

1. *A third resource was "public" input. In both revisions there were attempts made to allow input from the church at large. But these were not proficient, and what they elicited was regarded as advice to be heeded as the revisers saw fit. In truth, the majority of Anglicans were not keenly interested, and the revisers were (to use the classic American analogy) Hamiltonian democrats not Jeffersonian.*

the Carrington memorandum. The final rite would have been very different and inferior if it had simply been reproduced from the memorandum; instead, at one point or another, all those active in the Committee made significant contributions. Indeed, the revisers who met in Montreal after Christmas in 1953 (and before the memorandum had been received) had already begun many of the changes which gave 1962 its shape. But, as the minutes make very clear, the revisers were simply reacting to criticism: they had not formulated any clear-cut purpose, any positive goal to be achieved beyond that of responding to cries for change.

This was Carrington's great contribution (implied in the memorandum and expressed at the 1954 Congress): to provide the revision its underlying direction and motivation, the absence of which had led to much criticism in 1952. In the new world rushing to birth in the second half of the twentieth century, it was necessary for the Anglican Church of Canada to be integrated into a strong family of churches mutually identifiable by the faith and lifestyle expressed in the Prayer Book, and particularly in the liturgy which was at its heart. This was a goal whose legitimacy everyone could recognize and identify with, and in the years following, the Canadian revisers never wavered from it. The Canadian church emerged from the process of revision with a liturgy clearly belonging to the family of revised Anglican liturgies world-wide. It was, at the same time, a good expression of the life of the church in Canada in its day: 1552 in essence, but with compromises in the direction of 1549. It was basically conservative, making only changes that seemed necessary, and these as smoothly as possible. Even in the Prayer of Consecration, where the presence of a third paragraph was itself novel, the language was hallowed by custom and the phrasing remained familiar.

Indeed, so much remained familiar and customary that some complained 1962 was just more "tinkering with Cranmer." This was true to a degree, but in any responsible revision it was inevitable because of the organic nature of liturgy, which grows and evolves from the spiritual state and practice of the church that gives birth to it. One of the observed principles of human behaviour is that progress does not take place in leaps and bounds but by a steady evolution. Such gradual change may be traced so minutely (as was the case with much Near-Eastern pottery in the field of archaeology) that accurate and verifiable locations and dating sequences can be established. This principle is observable in society as well. Society manifests itself as a growth process, not as a static structure; and its laws nearly always presuppose a basis of existing custom and public opinion. Hence the maxim: "Only that which in some measure answers to a people's past has any power to mould that people's future."

What applies to human artifacts and social organization applies to liturgy as well — it is, traditionally, a product of custom.[1] What seems generally to be good and right is put into use for as long as it seems to be good and right. As usages evolve that better express the nature of the community, they gradually displace older forms.[2] Liturgy thus conceived is the outward expression of belief. From time to time it is codified (by Gregory VI, Alcuin, or Bishop Poore of Salisbury) but continues still to "grow" by being subject to local variation.

On the other hand, liturgy by statute law — freezing every comma in place — was a radical seventeenth-century departure. It blocked the slow but continuous growth by which usages most fit to express the faith were kept and others were allowed to pass away. Such immobilization of liturgy by statute law in England failed because, in spite of harsh penalties and the casting adrift of a large percentage of the population (even among the faithful), the law was unenforceable, and the inevitable process of selection went on however minutely or irregularly.[3] In a living community of faith, it remains true that "liturgiology ... actually goes on in churches not in books; written or printed liturgies are originally mere transcripts (probably imperfect) of what goes on in churches."[1] Revision, there-

---

1. Dix, op. cit., pp.716-719. Cf. also Carrington's remarks at the Congress, in Blott, op. cit., p.80.
2. An example in Anglican liturgy was the mandatory use of the Prayer of Humble Access while the Agnes Dei became optional.
3. Cf. above, p. 13 footnote 1.

fore, must begin at the grass roots, with an increasing awareness by the people of who they are and a deepening involvement in what they are doing; with the persuasion of clergy to take greater care in the preparation and leadership of worship; and with better education of seminarians and others in the nature and development of liturgy — the outward and visible form which clothes the inner spiritual reality.

In part, the fate of the 1952 revision was due to a failure to recognize the principle of organic growth. The "eleventh commandment" and the novel third paragraph of the Prayer of Consecration,[2] for example, show a freedom from tradition that was criticized as reckless disregard. This appears now to have been unfair to the revisers, but certainly 1952 was too much a product of its time.[3]

The 1952 rite, in its choice of "home-grown" elements over ones derived from traditional sources, may have been, for Canadian Anglicans, an assertion of nationalism. It reflected the surge of growth and development caused by World War II, and the self-confidence and energy of a country that had shot from a state of semi-colonial dependence to being one of the leading industrial nations of the world.[4] Unfortunately, it also exemplified one of the dangers foreseen at Lambeth in 1948 — namely, being caught up in the growth of domestic powers and capabilities to the detriment of an awareness of other liturgical developments that were not then able to influence the domestic process. There seemed to be no vision of the Canadian church as part of a whole that might be adversely affected by the church's actions and decisions. This self-confidence, energy, and freedom of action, however, gave the 1952 rite an-

---

1. The Most Rev. Philip Carrington, Draft of a letter to the Church Times in response to an article on the Canadian Prayer Book, dated Sept. 26, 1958, now with the Hallam Correspondence, General Synod Archives, Toronto, Ont.
2. Blott, op. cit., p. 99f.
3. At a time when the study of liturgics was still an esoteric one it would be unfair to judge the Canadian revisers by today's standards. In their time, they were among the most liturgically informed clergy in the Canadian church, and my interviews with the core group revealed a knowledge of the subject that would still be regarded as well-informed.
4. Cf. Canada: Nation on the March (Toronto, 1953).

other characteristic which, when looked at now, can be seen to have been ahead of its time. The greeting at the beginning of the rite, for example, and the spare wording of the third paragraph of the Prayer of Consecration, are not of the same genre as other rites of the era; they would fit in better today.[1]

The 1955 rite was a return to the traditional and, by virtue of its Prayer of Consecration, to the 1549 type of liturgy. In this sense, it fulfilled the dreams of Bishop Williams of Quebec, Dean Shreve, Archdeacon Vroom, and all the other post-1918 protagonists for revision of the liturgy. The majority of Canadian Anglicans would have accepted it. But for some, at the deep level of conscience, the theology of oblation in the Prayer of Consecration could simply not be tolerated; and once this was made clear, the prayer was modified. A high priority goal of the revisers and of most churchmen (as demonstrated by the outcome of the 1955 General Synod) was a traditional rite that all could use without reservation.

The 1955 rite (and its final 1962 form) revealed in the Canadian church a comprehensive spirit and a desire for solidarity. It was a codification of the belief and customs of Anglicans in Canada, or the "consensus fidelium," arrived at after two trial rites had allowed for the interaction of revisers and people.

The rite was not a new liturgy. In fact, to the contrary, it used traditional form and language; and rather than introducing new elements, it often gave official recognition to changes long desired and practised without sanction. It took no lead in the formation of contemporary liturgies, but brought the Canadian church solidly into step with the world-wide Anglican Communion. It was the last revision of the old Anglican lit-

---

1. It is ironic that the note of Palmer's apology for the 1952 addition to the Prayer of Consecration is being sounded again in relation to the composing of modern eucharistic prayers. cf. Geoffrey Cumming, "Four Very Early Anaphoras," Worship, Vol. 58, No.2 (March 1984) p.168f. The eucharistic prayer based on these models "would cease to be a kind of omnium gatherum," Cumming concludes. See also Louis Weil, "Opening Address to Eucharist 95," the meeting of the International Anglican Liturgical Consultation, Dublin, August 6-12, 1995.

urgy before the impact of modern scholarship and contemporary language created a whole new school of revisions; and it was the only modern revision of the 1552 type.

In the first half of the twentieth century, then, the Anglican Church of Canada produced a Canadian liturgy: a set of words and acts that gave outward expression to the relationship of this people with God. For the most part, this process moved just below the surface of the church's conscious mind — sometimes dropping out of sight, occasionally leaping up, but mostly staying in view of those who chose to look, and creating ripples here and there as it progressed.[1] In looking back to weigh and measure the accomplishment, though it is convenient to speak of separate acts, it must be recognized that there was only one revision: 1962 was a completion of the 1918 work.

In the first revision, the intention of the revisers was established by the Central Revision Subcommittee at the meeting of 20 April 1909. It was, as its reinforcement in 1911 showed, a victory for the Low Church party. They were able to keep out of the mandate any reference to the Solemn Declaration of 1893, whereby a way might have been opened for consideration, and perhaps adoption, of a more catholic faith and practice. The first revision, then, might be styled a Low Church revision, certainly not in comparison with the earlier revision of the Church of Ireland, but to the extent that the High Church party did not manage any changes of significance.

In consequence, the church as a whole gained a great deal. Against the distressing background of late nineteenth century quarrelling, and out of many misgivings, the 1918 Prayer Book

---

1. *The revisers sought to keep the public informed about the outcomes of their work and between October 16,1952, and November 1960, a series of 21 Articles by members of the Central Revision Sub-Committee was published in the* Canadian Churchman, *the national journal of the Anglican Church of Canada. Over the eight years, however, this brought forth only 61 letters. Most of the letters were from clergy (36) and only 15 were from lay-persons. The biggest response came regarding changes in the Calender (13 letters, 5 from laity) and there were eight letters concerning prayers for the departed. The biggest issue though was the Prayer of Consecration. Concern about this provoked 7 articles and 10 letters (all from clergy) and resulted in the substantial changes made to the prayer from its form in the 1955 draft book.*

emerged as solid evidence that the Canadian church could competently and safely carry through a reconsideration of this fundamental element in its nature, to the extent even of dealing successfully with that great thorn of nineteenth-century controversy, the Athanasian Creed. More specifically, a number of relevant services were added to meet the needs of the country.

Of little note at the time, but of great overall significance, was the restructuring of the liturgy by the abandoning of Cranmer's vision of an orthodox-type liturgy, and separating it into its constituent parts. This move cleared the ground of debate between the two theological schools in the church. The eighteenth-century informal revision, which allowed people simply to leave the liturgy early before its completion, was gone; and Morning Prayer now appeared as the legitimate competitor with the Holy Eucharist for recognition as the "regular Sunday service." Only in the ordinal was the old form of the liturgy retained by both the 1918 and 1962 revisers.

The second revision, if the old two-party terms of reference are adhered to, would probably have to be regarded as a victory for the High Churchmen, because they managed to have the eucharist considered. In that revision, the Ministry to the Sick was radically altered for the better, improvements were made in the baptism and marriage services, and all the revisers considered Cosgrave's work on the psalter to be one of the great achievements of the time. The eucharist, however, was its *raison d'etre*.

The general rubrics governing the liturgy were a matter of prolonged consideration resulting in the reinforcement of frequent communion and voluntary financial support of the church. Over the issue of the standards of behaviour to be expected and maintained in the church, however, the revisers declined to propose specific terms (as were found in 1549, in accordance with Cranmer's vision of the Christian community) and settled for general statements unlikely to lead to any of the particular consequences outlined in 1549.

The *synaxis* compared poorly with the daily offices as a piece of liturgy: the opening was still abrupt; the introduction of the introit and gradual psalms was made optional and was largely ignored; the decalogue remained an uncomfortable anomaly not clearly related to the rest of the rite; there was no Old Testament lesson; and the congregation was limited to "little responsories" except for the creed.

The Offertory, Thanksgiving, and Consecration, however, fared much better. In the selection of sentences, and by rubrical direction, the Offertory was restored as an offering of life in the presentation of bread and wine, which might be brought to the altar by members of the congregation. The expansion of the *Vere Dignum* not only introduced, at this point, the basic relationship between God and humanity, it also set the precedent for later additions. More Proper Prefaces were included, the Peace was restored to its customary medieval place, and the Prayer of Humble Access returned to where it had been in 1549. The Our Father remained after communion.

The revision's greatest achievement was the additional paragraph in the Prayer of Consecration produced under the direction of Archbishop Clark for the 1955 draft book. Its theology can be summed up in the concluding paragraph of his preface to the book: the Holy Eucharist is done by those who, by water and the spirit, have been joined to Christ and have begun the new life. When two or more of them gather together in his name to "do this," they join with Christ in his eternal self-offering before God. The new creation of the Word joins in his perfect response to the Creator, whose loving Spirit, as so long ago, moves through the void of darkness upon the deep, and brings forth light and life. Wherefore:

> O Father ... we ... remember before thee the precious death, the mighty resurrection, and the glorious ascension of thy beloved Son; And looking for his coming again in glory, we present unto thy divine Majesty this holy Bread of eternal life and this Cup of everlasting salvation.... And we pray that by the power of thy Holy Spirit, all we who are partakers of this holy Communion may be fulfilled with thy grace and heavenly benediction....

The *epiclesis* was never strongly worded, but the loss of the oblation in the final form of the rite was a major failure in the revision, and meant that, in spite of appearing more tradi-tional, the Prayer of Consecration was still substantially that of the 1552 model. The loss of the oblation came about because of a failure to understand the eucharist as an act deriving from baptism and dependent on what was accomplished in baptism. The best that could be said (and this much was intended) was that the 1962 wording was sufficiently ambiguous that it could be interpreted as orthodox.

A great gain, however, in the Canadian church was the removal of the eucharist from its position with the occasional offices, the position Hague had used to bolster his interpretation of the liturgy as non-sacramental. The move demonstrated what synods and bishops were now asserting — that the eucharist was the central act of Christian worship. This assertion itself brought the Anglican Church of Canada into line with ecumenical thinking and with the world-wide Communion of Anglicans. Even though, a quarter of a century later, the eucharist as the central act of Christian worship has not yet been fully actualized, the principle has been clearly established and remains only to be worked out in due time.

The 1962 revision of the Prayer Book was the end of an era. Out of its Tudor and Caroline roots, out of the strivings of Wesley and Simeon, out of the electrifying Tractarian campaign (the theological battles and ritual confrontations) — and by debate and compromise, and patience — the Anglican Communion, and the Canadian church with it, had at last arrived at an answer to the question posed at the Reformation: "How do I work out my salvation from day to day?" The old answer found in Acts 2:42 had been right all along; what had been wrong was the legalistic and mechanical implementation of the teaching. The sacraments were, as always, the normal means of grace and the hope of glory, and while "the breaking of bread and the prayers" had been brought into touch with the nature of the community, the aspect of "the apostle's teaching and fellowship" (the *synaxis*) had not fared as well. The role of the individual within the congregation had yet to be restored with her or his act of faith and psychological responses, but how that could be accomplished lay far beyond the purview of revision in the first half of the century. Its realization would come in the future.

The basic problem was — and is — that, for over a thousand years, the liturgical model has depicted "professional ministers" administering to a group of "lay clients" who more or less passively accept what the leaders provide. The almost complete passivity of the people in the liturgy at the end of the Middle Ages was somewhat improved upon in England at the Reformation, in that they could hear and see what was done, approach the altar, and respond in chorus. The model, however, remained the same, with the professional leader administering to his clients. The job ahead would be to develop a new model of corporate action that would allow both individual and group initiative and response involving all the physical senses, in order to reach deeply to pluck the chords of archetypal symbols and drives basic to being human. In short, the way of the future is to develop a model of corporate worship that, by all these means, proclaims the gospel to the whole person and to all people. To begin on this work, Christians must be made aware of the inadequacy of the old priest-client model, and become involved in the development of a new model of liturgy. This has been the underlying purpose of the bulk of liturgical work since the end of the 1950s, and has raised the even more basic question: "How is one saved?"

In the last decade of the twentieth century this is becoming the focus of attention.

Bibliography

Abbott-Smith, The Reverend G. Letter to The Right Reverend Philip Carrington, on the subject of Prayer Book revision, dated November 29, 1938. Armitage Papers, Wycliffe College, Toronto.

Letters to the Rt. Rev. W.T. Hallam on the subject of his resignation as secretary, dated July 19 & Sept. 28, 1939. Armitage Papers, Wycliffe College, Toronto.

Acton, Lord John E., editor. *Lectures on Modern History*. London: Collins, 1960.

Anon. *Vital Questions for Canadian Churchmen*. General Synod Archives, Toronto.

Armitage, The Rev. Dr. Ramsey. "Canadian Prayer Book Revision." *Pan Anglican*. Vol. IV, No. 2 (Oct. 1953).

Letter to the Rt. Rev. W.T. Hallam on the subject of Anglican Action, dated July 29, 1954. Armitage Papers, Wycliffe College, Toronto.

Letters to the Rt. Rev. W.T. Hallam on the subject of changes in drafts of the Prayer Book, dated 1952-1955. Armitage Papers, Wycliffe College, Toronto.

Letter to the Rt. Rev. W.T. Hallam on the subject of Committee procedure, dated March 6, 1950. Armitage Papers, Wycliffe College, Toronto.

Three letters to the Rt. Rev. W.T. Hallam on the subject of membership of the Central Revision Sub-Committee, dated 1953-1955. Armitage Papers, Wycliffe College, Toronto.

Armitage, W.J. *The Story of the Canadian Revision of the Prayer Book.* Toronto: McClelland and Stewart Ltd., 1922.

Blott, William R. "The Influence of the Most Reverend Philip Carrington, Archbishop of Quebec in revising the Liturgy of the Book of Common Prayer 1959 Canada," unpublished M.A. thesis.

Book of Common Prayer and Administration of the Sacraments and Other Rites and Ceremonies of the Church According to the Use of the Anglican Church of Canada, The. Toronto: The Anglican Book Centre, 1959.

Book of Common Prayer and Administration of the Sacraments and Other Rites and Ceremonies of the Church According to the Use of the Church of England in The Dominion of Canada. Toronto: Cambridge University Press.

Book of Common Prayer and Administration of the Sacraments and Other Rites and Ceremonies of the Church Together with the Form and Manner of Making, Ordaining and Consecrating of Bishops, Priests and Deacons, Set Forth by Authority for Use in the Church of the Province of South Africa. London: Oxford University Press, 1954.

Buchanan, Colin, Trevor Lloyd & Harold Miller, eds. *Anglican Worship Today.* London: Collins Liturgical Publications, 1980.

The End Of The Offertory — An Anglican Study. Bramcote, Notts: Grove Books, 1978.

What Did Cranmer Think He Was Doing? Bramcote, Notts: Grove Books, 1976.

Buxton, Richard F. *Eucharist and Institution Narrative.* London: S.P.C.K., 1976.

Canada: *Nation on the March.* Toronto: Clarke, Irwin Company Ltd., 1953.

Carrington, The Most Rev. Philip. Draft of a letter to the *Church Times* in response to an article on the Canadian Prayer Book, dated Sept. 26, 1958. Hallam Correspondence, General Synod Archives, Toronto.

Letter to the Rt. Rev. W.T. Hallam on the subject of revision principles, dated Nov. 13, 1943. Armitage Papers, Wycliffe College, Toronto.

The Anglican Church in Canada. Toronto: Collins, 1963.

Central Revision Sub-Committee of the Joint Committee of the General Synod on the Enrichment and Adaptation of the *Book of Common Prayer.* Minutes of September 13, 1911.

Chadwick, Owen. *The Reformation.* Harmondsworth: Penguin Books, 1964.

Clark, The Most. Rev. Howard H. Interview given to the author on the subject of Prayer Book revision at his home in Toronto, on Sept. 19, 1977.

Letter to the Archbishops, Bishops and Clergy, The Anglican Church of Canada, dated Feb. 20, 1957. Hallam Correspondence, General Synod Archives, Toronto.

Prayer Book Revision in Canada Toronto: General Synod Archives, 1958.

Cockshut, A.O.J. *Anglican Attitudes: A Study of Victorian Religious Controversies.* London: Collins, 1959.

Committee of the Lower House of the Convocation of Canterbury on the Royal Letter of Business of Nov. 10, 1906. The Ornaments Rubric and Modifications of the Existing Law Relating to the Conduct of Divine Service. Report No. 428. London: 1909.

Cragg, Gerald R. *The Church and the Age of Reason 1648-1789.* Hammondsworth: Penguin Books, 1970.

Cross, F.L. editor. *The Oxford English Dictionary.* London: Oxford U. Press, 1958.

Cuming, Geoffrey. "Four Very Early Anaphoras," *Worship.* Vol.58, No. 2 (Mar. 1984).

Dix, Gregory. *The Shape of the Liturgy.* Westminster: Dacre Press, 1945.

General Committee on Revision of the *Book of Common Prayer.* Minute Books A, B, C, I, II & III. General Synod Archives, Toronto.

General Synod of the Church of England in the Dominion of Canada. Convening Circular for the Fifth Session 1908. General Synod Archives, Toronto.

General Synod of the Church of England in Canada. Journal of Proceedings ... 1896 - 1952. General Synod Archives, Toronto.

Hague, Dyson. *The Holy Communion of the Church of England.* London, undated.

The Protestantism of the Prayer Book. Toronto: 1890.

Through the Prayer Book. London: Longmans Greens, & Co., 1932.

Hallam, The Rt. Rev. W.T. Draft of a letter to the Rev. Roland F. Palmer, on the subject of the Prayer of Consecration, dated "after September/before Toronto meeting 1954." Armitage Papers, Wycliffe College, Toronto.

Draft of a letter to the Rev Roland F. Palmer, on the subject of the revision of the eucharist, in reply to a letter of Aug. 14, 1951. Armitage Papers, Wycliffe College, Toronto.

Draft of a third paragraph for the Prayer of Consecration. Armitage Papers, Wycliffe College, Toronto.

Letter to the Rt. Rev. Sir Francis Heathcote on the subject of Prayer Book revision, dated Oct. 21, 1943. Armitage Papers, Wycliffe College, Toronto.

Letter to the Rev. Dr. Ramsey Armitage on the subject of Committee minutes, dated Oct. 21, 1943. Armitage Papers, Wycliffe College, Toronto.

Hatchett, Marion J. *Sanctifying Life, Time and Space.* New York: Seabury Press, 1976.

Headon, Christopher Fergus. "The Influence of the Oxford Movement Upon the Church of England in Eastern and Central Canada, 1840 - 1900." Unpublished Ph.D. thesis.

Jasper, R.C.D. *Prayer Book Revision in England 1800-1900.* London: S.P.C.K., 1954.

Joint Committee of General Synod on the Appendix to the *Book of Common Prayer.* Proposed Appendix to the *Book of Common Prayer.* Anglican Church of Canada, 1905.

Joint Committee of the General Synod of Canada on the Enrichment and Adaptation of the *Book of Common Prayer.* Minute Book. General Synod Archives, Toronto.

Lambeth Conference, The. Conference of Bishops of the Anglican Communion: Holden at Lambeth Palace July 6 to August 5, 1908. London: S.P.C.K., 1908.

The Encyclical Letter from the Bishops; together with Resolutions and Reports. London: S.P.C.K., 1948.

Massey, Hamilton Shepherd Jr. *The Oxford American Prayer Book Commentary.* New York: Oxford University Press, 1950.

Matheson, the Most Rev. S.P. Letter to the Ven W.J. Armitage on the subject of the Prayer Book, undated, now with the Revision Committee correspondence. General Synod Archives, Toronto.

Michell, G.A. *Landmarks in Liturgy.* London: Darton, Longman and Todd, 1961.

Mockridge, Charles H. *The Bishops of the Church of England in Canada and Newfoundland.* Toronto: F.N.W. Brown, 1896.

Morison, Samuel Eliot. *The Oxford History of the American People.* New York: Oxford University Press, 1965.

Neil, Charles and J.M. Willoughby, editors. *The Tutorial Prayer Book.* London: Church Book Room Press Ltd., 1963.

Palmer, The Rev. Roland F. Interview given to the author on the subject of Prayer Book revision, at his home in Toronto, August 22, 1977.

Letter to the Rev. M.C.S. Hutt, *Canadian Churchman.* Vol. 80, No. 1 (Jan. 1, 53).

Letter to the Rt. Rev. W.T. Hallam, on the subject of the Prayer of Consecration, dated April 20, 1950. Armitage Papers, Wycliffe College, Toronto.

Letter to the Rt. Rev. W.T. Hallam on the subject of the revision of the eucharist, dated June 19, 1951. Armitage Papers, Wycliffe College, Toronto.

Letter to the Rt. Rev. W.T. Hallam on the subject of revision of the eucharist, dated Aug. 14, 1951. Armitage Papers, Wycliffe College, Toronto.

Letter to the Rt. Rev. W.T. Hallam on the subject of the Prayer of Consecration, dated Aug. 1, 1954. Armitage Papers, Wycliffe College, Toronto.

"Prayer Book Revision." *Queens College Occasional Paper.* No. 2 (May 1955).

Potter, Alonzo, ed. *The Memorial Papers.* Philadelphia: E.H. Butler & Co., 1857.

Prayer Book Studies IV, *The Eucharistic Liturgy.* New York: Church Pension Fund, 1953.

Proctor, Francis and W.H. Frere. *A New History of the Book of Common Prayer.* London: MacMillan & Co. 1961.

Report of Action taken by the Provincial Synod of the Ecclesiastical Province of Canada on the Revised Prayer Book, Oct. 2, 1917.

Report of the Secretary of the Joint Committee of Both Houses on the Adaptation, Enrichment and Revision of the Book of Common Prayer with Resolutions Prepared in due Form Covering All the Adaptation, Enrichments and Revisions Proposed by the Committee. London: Cambridge University Press, 1914.

Seaborn, The Most Rev. Robert. Interview given to the author on the subject of Prayer Book Revision at Sundridge, Aug. 20, 1980.

Short, The Rt. Rev. H.V.R. Letter to the author on the subject of the acceptance of the Report on the Prayer Book by General Synod in 1959, dated Jan. 12, 1978.

Shreve, Richmond. *The Prayer of Consecration in the Holy Communion Office*. St. Johns: The E.R. Smith Co. Ltd., 1920.

Sub-Committee of the Joint Committee of the General Synod on the Enrichment and Adaptation of the Book of Common Prayer. Minutes, April 20, 1909. General Synod Archives, Toronto.

Trevelyan, G.M. *Illustrated History of England*. London: Longmans, 1945.

Tripp, David H. E.C. *Ratcliff: Reflexions on Liturgical Revision*. Bramcote: Grove Books, 1980.

Tuchman, Barbara W. *The Guns of August*. New York: MacMillan Publishing Co., 1962.

Vidler, Alec R. *The Church in an Age of Revolution*. Hammondsworth: Penguin Books, 1961.

Vroom, F.W. *An Introduction to the Prayer Book*. London: S.P.C.K., 1930.

Prayer Book Revision in Canada: Lectures Delivered at the Summer School for Clergy at King's College, Windsor, N.S., dated 1915. General Synod Archives, Toronto.

Walsh, H.H. *The Christian Church in Canada*. Toronto: The Ryerson Press, 1956.

Wigan, Bernard. *The Liturgy in English*. London: Oxford University Press, 1962.

Williams, The Rt. Rev. David. Letter to the Ven. W.J. Armitage on the subject of the Prayer Book, dated March 26, 1927. Revision Committee correspondence, General Synod Archives, Toronto.

Winspear, W.W. Letter to the Rt. Rev. J.C. Farthing on the subject of further Prayer Book revision, dated Feb. 24, 1938. Armitage Papers, Wycliffe College, Toronto.